SAVE THAT HOUSE

A homeowner's guide to prevention
and control of insect and decay
damage in wooden buildings

By A.J. HUPP

D. & J. PUBLISHING COMPANY
SHELTON, WASHINGTON

COPYRIGHT © 1983 By A.J. HUPP

LIBRARY OF CONGRESS CATALOG CARD
No. 83-72006

ISBN 0-9611744-0-4

First Printing April, 1984

Printed in the United States of America
by Litho Art Printing
Portland, Oregon

Art Work and Photographs by A.J. Hupp
Shelton, Washington

D. & J. Publishing Company
S.E. 261 Brigham Court
Shelton, Washington, 98584

TABLE OF CONTENTS

INTRODUCTION

As high interest rates and periods of excessive inflation push new home costs out of reach, many Americans are turning to alternatives. One of the most popular choices is the purchase and restoration of a "fixer-upper." The end result can be an economical and satisfying experience, or an absolute disaster. Much of the outcome depends on how well we understand what we are getting into. The trick is to find out what's wrong with the house, and then decide if its problems can be corrected at a reasonable price.

Of course that assumes we are working with a knowledge base that allows us to correctly evaluate the building's condition. Yet most of us are a bit deficient when it comes to passing judgement on the condition of a house. We are also at some disadvantage when it comes to recognizing design and construction errors that can allow even new buildings to deteriorate.

For me, upgrading that deficient knowledge base was a long, laborious, and frustrating experience because finding the information was difficult. The question to be answered was: "What makes some buildings vulnerable to insect attack and decay, while others seem to stand forever?" I found the book stores and local libraries stuffed with how-to-do-it information on carpentry, plumbing, and landscaping, but very little material on the root causes of wooden building deterioration.

So the information in the following chapters was dug from the bowels of university libraries, and extracted from the minds of professors, contractors, county extension agents, exterminators, lumber industry executives, and home remodeling experts. And this text intends to arm homeowners with more facts than are normally available on how insects and decay destroy wooden buildings.

This book should also increase the value of your do-it-yourself library collection because it solves many of the mysteries introduced by more technical books on carpentry, remodeling, plumbing, insulation, roofing, and landscaping.

CHAPTER 1

DECAY AND INSECT PROBLEMS ARE SERIOUS

SERIOUS BUILDING DECAY

FIG 1-1

If we use dollar costs as a measurement, insect activity and decay are more serious than fire. According to Department of Agriculture statistics, bugs and rot cause more structural damage annually than flame.

TYPICAL CASES

For one Virginia homeowner, his contractor's understanding of building code philosophy and local conditions paid off. Even at the 20 year point, the house shows no signs of deterioration, though it is located where subterranean termites

and decay are significant problems. But his do-it-yourself tool shed, figure 1-1, serves as a constant reminder that improperly constructed wooden buildings can be rendered useless in less than 5 years.

Several simple errors caused the shed's sad condition. Proper drainage was denied to the roof area because of inadequate slope. An insufficient eave overhang exposed the upper walls to moisture. Wood had also been placed too close to the damp ground with insufficient circulation under the floor joists. The end result was advanced decay in the upper walls and outer rafter ends, along with a floor structure powdered by termite and ant activity.

Maintenance neglect contributed to the shed's deterioration as well. An accumulation of leaves and other vegetation provided a direct path to structural wood for insects and decay fungi.

Another case involves the owner of a 50-year-old house in Washington State where significant dampwood termite problems exist. Due to its age, the structure conformed to few modern building codes, but where codes had been applied, the house was still sound. Had it not been for serious maintenance neglect over the years, the building could have been reconditioned and saved. But termites had eaten away the floor and wall area around the bathroom. They, along with carpenter ants, had destroyed the structural integrity of an entire back wall. All other outside walls had major decay resulting from inadequate eave overhang and roof gutter disrepair. Powder post beetles had entered the house with the original rough-cut lumber and destroyed many major support beams.

These two cases are typical of what home-owners may find in the way of protection from insects and decay. But even a worst case should not generate panic. A mature termite colony of 60,000 members can only eat about a fifth of an ounce of wood per day.

WHAT DEGREE OF PROTECTION SHOULD WE EXPECT?

The protection afforded us ranges from none to nearly 100 percent and depends on many factors including design, location, cost, and maintenance.

According to Department of Agriculture figures, less than one percent of American homes receive chemical protection against termites. On the other hand, significant mechanical protection is provided by adhering to local and national building codes during construction. In fact, structural preservation is one of the primary reasons building codes were created in the first place. That should give us cause to make certain the codes are used and improved upon. However, not all construction methods, materials, or building practices give good protection even though technically correct. In some geographical locations and prevailing weather conditions, we must use extraordinary measures to protect wooden structures.

Probably the best answer to the question of how much protection you can expect is to anticipate none and be pleasantly surprised on your next inspection.

WHAT ABOUT CHEMICAL PROTECTION?

A few years back we thought we had the insect problem solved with chemicals. Commonly, chemical barriers were laid around buildings and expected to last up to 30 years. But more and more, health authorities are uncovering instances where surface water and underground wells have been contaminated by chemicals used to protect buildings. Other instances are coming to light where the buildings themselves are health hazards because the ground underneath is saturated with long-life insecticides. It has taken years to understand some of these problems and it may take many more years before the entire picture develops.

Along the same line, chemically treated wood affords better protection than untreated wood and building codes call for treated wood in many places. Yet we may not know the full story on chemically treated wood either. For that reason, this book emphasizes mechanical prevention and de-emphasizes the use of chemicals. Mechanical means will not solve all our problems, but until we understand more on the chemical aspect, we should be very cautious about what we use and how it is applied.

SUMMARY

While national statistics are interesting, they are of little value in determining the severity of building deterioration in any particular case. After reading the following chapters, you should be able to thoroughly inspect a structure and determine how serious the situation is. You should also be able to make one of the following comments about its condition:

1. Oh boy, I had no idea!

2. It could be worse!

3. No problem yet, but now I know what to look for and I'll keep looking.

Additionally, you should be able to decide what mechanical steps are required to correct an undesirable condition and determine if chemical application is necessary to prevent future problems.

We do not intend to make you an expert carpenter, exterminator, entomologist, or building inspector, but we do intend to acquaint you with those fields to a considerable depth. We expect that you will know enough to recognize when you need to talk with a real expert and that you will be able to evaluate his or her advice as it applies to your situation.

From the homeowner's standpoint, building deterioration is serious, as in figure 1-2. It may not generate adrenaline like the word FIRE, but the end result will be similar if important signals and conditions are overlooked or ignored.

BUILDING DETERIORATION

FIG 1-2

CHAPTER 2

WOOD-DESTROYING INSECTS
(and others)

Worldwide, we contend with wood-destroying insects by the thousands. Fortunately, only a few consistently chew up our homes. In the United States, we are primarily concerned with subterranean termites, drywood termites, dampwood termites, powder post beetles, and carpenter ants. The following pages present considerable detail on these insects because understanding them is prerequisite to developing effective control and elimination programs.

Additionally, we are bothered by pests which contaminate food, chew up books, destroy clothing, and create a general nuisance. Some are erroneously associated with wood-destroying activity as well. We commonly find silver fish, firebrats, sow bugs, pill bugs, and earwigs in or near deteriorated wood and assume these insects are the cause. Not so. They are only innocent bystanders where home destruction is concerned. Nonetheless, we will examine their habits as related to our central issue of wood deterioration.

INSECT IDENTIFICATION

Improperly identifying our wood-destroying culprits can lead to costly and frustrating mistakes, and it is not only homeowners who can be misled by erroneous assumptions. A Florida man who discovered termites in his kitchen floor provides a case in point.

Assuming the termites were subterranean, he proceeded with an extensive and expensive elimination program. He knew that subterranean termites must maintain routes between wood and soil. Finding no obvious subterranean termite shelter tubes, he exposed the entire foundation for inspection. Still finding no shelter tubes, he assumed the termites were traveling through foundation cracks or inside the wood itself. So he removed all wood in contact with, or close to, the soil and sealed all foundation wall cracks. Thinking the problem was solved, he repaired the damaged kitchen area. Guess what he found the next year. Termite damage in the new wood.

Exasperated, he called an exterminator who chemically treated the foundation area for subterranean termites. Even then, termite activity continued.

That's when he became serious about determining exactly what his troublesome insects were. All research findings pointed toward dampwood rather than subterranean termites. They were living entirely within the structure without soil contact. The colony's moisture needs were being satisfied by cold-water pipe condensation drips. After he rerouted and insulated the pipe, the area dried up and the termites died. (All termites are really very fragile things and highly susceptible to even minor environmental changes.) He would have been time, money, and effort ahead had be been able to properly identify the insects in the first place.

I don't mean to imply that insect identification is easy. It is not. We can seldom create laboratory conditions in insect-infested buildings because key elements can not be isolated or controlled. Most often, we can't even capture the insects for study. If structural deterioration has progressed significantly, we are commonly dealing with more than one insect type. The situation may be further complicated by wood decay and its associated insects. Routinely, we see a complicated mess created by carpenter ants and powder post beetles crossing paths in the wood with termite galleries and rot on top of it all. The point is illustrated by figure 2-1.

DETERIORATED WOOD

FIG 2-1

To a casual observer, the photograph represents nothing more than rotten boards. Yes, decay is the predominant feature, but there are others. The board's original form has been significantly altered by insect action. Some bugs have left smooth and clean lines while others produced jagged fractures. A more microscopic examination reveals insect leavings including excrement, wings, and carcasses. Notice a dead sow bug located 3/4 of an inch below the round knot in the photograph. He was not contributing to deterioration, only cleaning up previous decay. But he is part of the confusing mess.

So with the intent of reducing confusion and increasing our ability to identify wood-destroying insects, let us examine our most famous character.

TERMITES IN GENERAL

Termites stand near the bottom of the insect life scale in close relationship to cockroaches and grasshoppers. Like cockroaches, termites have been around for about 350 million years.

Entomologists have identified almost 2,000 ter-

mite species, so it is neither possible nor desirable to treat species individually in a book of this nature. Instead, we use three general classifications which are well-suited to the homeowner's task of identifying and eliminating termites.

Subterranean termites are the best known and are followed in notoriety by the dampwood and drywood classifications.

Throughout this section we will use the subterranean type as a basic reference on characteristics and habits. Where dampwood and drywood termites differ from subterraneans, we will so note as we go along.

TERMITE CONCENTRATION IN THE UNTIED STATES

As indicated in figure 2-2, most termite attacks are concentrated in the southeastern states and western California. But they are common enough throughout the rest of our country to cause nearly everyone some concern.

The eastern subterranean termite is the most destructive and it is common in, but not limited to,

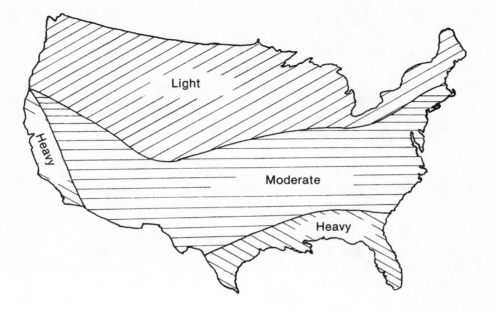

FREQUENCY OF TERMITE ATTACK

FIG 2-2

northeastern states. We must deal with eastern subterranean, western subterranean or arid land subterranean termites in every state except Alaska.

Dampwood termite problems are mostly in the coastal areas and damp climates.

Drywood termites are generally located where humidity is low, but also cause considerable concern from Cape Henry to the Florida Keys and along the Gulf Coast. In our highly mobile society, drywood termites sometimes move along with our household goods and find suitable survival conditions in unlikely geographical areas. For example, we would not expect to find drywood termites in Tacoma, Washington because of the damp climate, yet the insect has been found there. Drywood termites may survive long distance moves because they do not depend on soil contact or damp wood for moisture.

Many homeowners overlook termite damage because their locale has a termite free reputation. We should guard against being led into a false sense of security just because neighbors would

have us believe termites are not a problem. We should find out for ourselves by looking carefully at *our* homes.

WHY SO MUCH CONCERN OVER THIS THING CALLED "TERMITE"?

The termite has such a terrible reputation that we even blame him for damage caused by other insects and rot. Part of his reputation stems from his basic nature because he sneaks around in the dark, doing severe damage before detection. Actual termite sightings are rare even after their presence is known and we tend to fear what we cannot see. Further, the termite's reputation is capitalized on and perpetuated by the extermination industry in advertisements.

DAN'S EXTERMINATION SERVICE
**"What you don't know
can hurt your home."**
CALL TODAY 023-555-3777

Notice the word "TERMITE" was not used in

the advertisement, but the thought likely came to mind anyway. So we are conditioned to think "TERMITE" when considering extermination services and building deterioration.

Unfortunately, so much emphasis is placed on termites that we may overlook powder post beetles and carpenter ants. In actuality, powder post beetles do nearly as much harm as termites. Yet many readers will learn about them for the first time in the following pages. Termites, carpenter ants, and powder post beetles are all bad characters and should be well-understood by the homeowner. We should also understand what they are not.

THE TERMITE IS NOT AN ANT

Commonly, we hear folks talk about termites as "just another form of flying white ant". The argument goes like this: "Flying ants have two sets of transparent wings, as do termites. Both insects swarm during summer months and fly around looking for nesting places. There are color similarities. Both insects can be found nesting in, and destroying wood. Therefore termites must be a specific form of flying ant." But the argument falls apart when we realize the two insects are deadly enemies and don't even look alike.

Viewing figure 2-3, we see the termite's head is pointed at the mouth with eyes set well forward. The ant's eyes set on the back third of a rather egg-shaped head.

Termite antennae form a continuous curved line and are jointed only at the head. Ant antennae are jointed at the head and additionally form an elbow at mid-length. The ant antennae form a sickle shape, and curve in the opposite direction from those of the termite.

Ants have a very narrow restriction at the waist where termites have none.

All six of the termite's legs are uniformly distributed along each side of the entire body length. The ant's legs are concentrated in the forward part of the body, above the waistline.

Another distinguishing feature separating ants from termites is found in the wing structure. Notice the leading edge of the termite wing in figure 2-3. There is a smooth clean area between the edge and the first section of vein patterns below it. Now look at the ant wing. The ant wing "stigma" is located in an area that would be blank if the wing belonged to a termite. In some ant species, detection of the "stigma" must be made with a magnifying glass.

Termite wings normally have three distinctly defined vein pattern sections while the vein pattern in ant wings is more open and random. There are also fewer and larger veins in the ant's wings.

All four termite wings are quite similar in size, shape, and pattern. On the ant, the forward wings are larger than the aft set and the two sets may have very different vein patterns.

When held up to the light, ant wings are transparent in comparison with the more translucent termite wings.

All of this comparison should lead to the conclusion that termites are not simply another form of ant. Yet, there are many who try to rid their homes of termites by using ant baits, poisons, and traps. As long as they believe termites are actually ants, they persist in one ineffective method after another. Meanwhile, the houses continue to deteriorate.

TERMITE COMMUNITY LIFE

Suberranean termite colonies have three cast members which are all different in appearance.

REPRODUCTIVES — During early colony development, the sexual adult king and queen do all the work. They reproduce, maintain a suitable habitat, provide food and water, and care for the young. As the colony enlarges, some offspring develop into workers, others become soldiers, and a few are groomed into secondary reproductives. Eventually the king and queen do nothing but reproduce and the queen becomes so large she can't even move. Reproductives have a much higher physical development than workers or soldiers. Unlike the soldier and worker castes, reproductives have compound eyes and can see. Primary reproductives also sprout wings for use in the swarming process.

Swarming provides man with frequent opportunities to observe the reproductive caste of all termite species. Through such observations, we are given clues to help identify termite types.

Western subterranean reproductives are black with gray wings while the eastern variety ranges in color from yellowish to dark gray.

Reproductive drywood termites are light yellow, dark brown or blackish with reddish heads.

Dampwood reproductives are dark brown, including the wings. The Pacific dampwood species is distinguished by a large, dark reddish brown head, figures 2-4 and 2-5.

COMPARISON OF TERMITE AND ANT

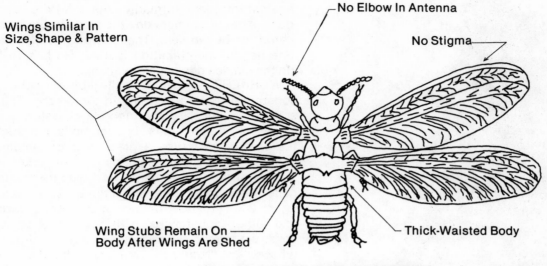

Wings Similar In Size, Shape & Pattern

No Elbow In Antenna

No Stigma

Wing Stubs Remain On Body After Wings Are Shed

Thick-Waisted Body

WINGED ADULT TERMITE

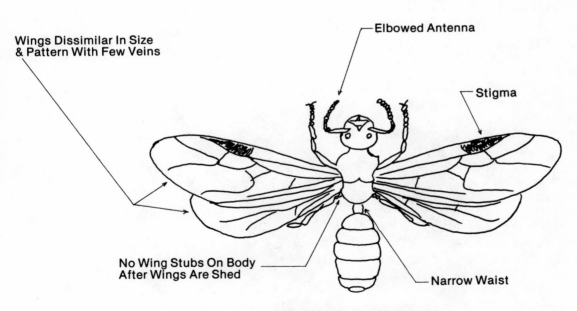

Wings Dissimilar In Size & Pattern With Few Veins

Elbowed Antenna

Stigma

No Wing Stubs On Body After Wings Are Shed

Narrow Waist

WINGED ADULT ANT

FIG 2-3

WINGED ADULT TERMITE

FIG 2-4

SOLDIERS — As depicted in figure 2-6, soldiers have large heads with pincers in front. Although blind, the soldier's function is to guard its colony against intruders, primarily ants. Like the reproductive caste, soldiers do little work and must be cared for by workers. The drywood soldier has one helpful identification feature. He has teeth on the inside edges of his pincers.

WORKERS — Numerically, blind workers constitute the largest caste in the colony. They enlarge the nest, gather food and water, and construct shelter tubes. In accomplishing such tasks, workers cause a great deal of building damage. The most significant distinguishing feature of the subterranean worker is its "fontanelle" or secretion pore in the center of its head, figure 2-7. The subterranean worker mixes earth and other substances with its secretion to construct termite shelter tubes or tunnels. Shelter tubes will be discussed in a moment, but it should be noted here that only subterranean workers build them.

NYMPHS — There are no worker castes, as such, in drywood or dampwood termite colonies. In both cases, worker functions are performed by developing sexual adults (nymphs) and sometimes by soldiers.

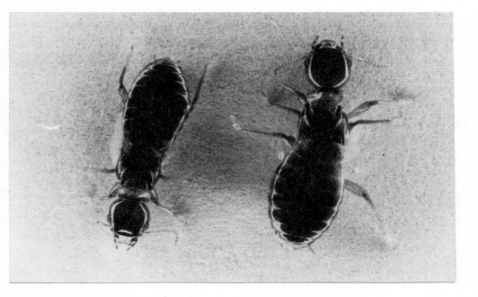

WINGLESS ADULT TERMITES

FIG 2-5

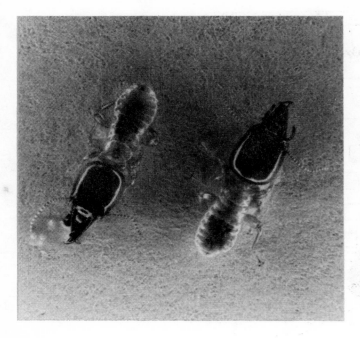

SOLDIER TERMITES

FIG 2-6

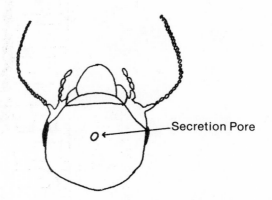

Secretion Pore

SUBTERRANEAN
TERMITE WORKER

Fig 2-7

Dampwood termite nymphs can be identified by dark spots on the abdomen. The spots are caused by intestinal contents which show through the outer skin as can be seen in figure 2-8.

TERMITES MUST HAVE WATER

Subterranean, drywood, and dampwood termites all obtain water in different ways. Once we discover how a particular colony gets its moisture, we have taken a significant step toward identifying the type.

Eliminating the water source or preventing travel between water and food is an important element of control when dealing with subterranean and dampwood termites. However, little can be done to deprive drywood termites of moisture.

DRYWOOD TERMITE MOISTURE REQUIREMENTS — Drywood termites gain sufficient water from feeding material but their environmental humidity must be very carefully controlled for survival. The way they accomplish humidity control gives us an important identifying clue.

DAMPWOOD
TERMITE NYMPH

FIG 2-8

17

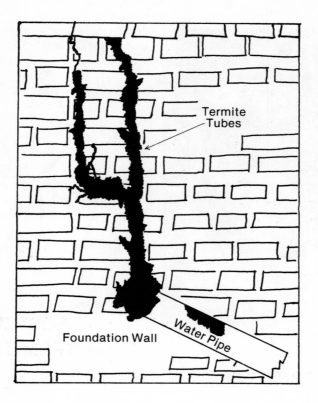

Termite Tubes

Foundation Wall

Water Pipe

TERMITE TUBES ON FOUNDATION WALL

FIG 2-9

Unlike other types, drywood termites chew humidity control holes out through the surfaces of infested wood. The holes are then sealed over with a blackish or brownish secretion which hardens into paper-thin plugs. These plugs are visible and often look like surface blisters on the wood.

Because drywood termites depend on no outside moisture source, their initial attacks often come at the upper wall or roof level. They are very difficult to eliminate or even control without extermination chemicals.

SUBTERRANEAN TERMITE MOISTURE REQUIREMENTS — For the most part, subterranean termite colonies must remain in the ground to satisfy moisture requirements. Colony movement will occur underground if moisture conditions change permanently or soil temperature varies significantly. With temporarily changing conditions, workers range quite far to bring water to other colony members. In excessively wet soil, the colony may perish if it cannot escape to a more suitable environment.

When sufficient food and water are found underground, the colony's essential survival requirements are met and they have no need to enter buildings.

DAMPWOOD TERMITE MOISTURE REQUIREMENTS — As the name implies, dampwood termite moisture needs are satisfied by the wood they feed on. Ground contact is not necessary, and they often live entirely within infested wood as long as it remains damp. They commonly enter houses through wood in contact with the soil, but not always. Once the colony is well established, its activity may extend into relatively dry wood, but moisture in the area remains necessary.

SUBTERRANEAN TERMITE SHELTER TUBES

When subterranean termites feed above ground, they must construct shelter tubes to protect themselves from dehydration through air exposure. Workers and soldiers are very susceptible to dehydration while the reproductives have a high tolerance for light and exposure.

In shelter tube construction, subterranean termites use particles of earth, wood, and other debris. The tubes are very irregular and more flat against the surface than round in shape, as indicated by figure 2-9. Tube width varies from one-quarter to over half an inch. Shelter tube color and strength are dictated by the soil type used for construction. These tubes may be built inside, outside, or within foundation walls.

No matter how much food is found at the end of the tube, subterraneans must return to soil for moisture and therefore the tubes must be maintained.

Shelter tubes built in the open are easily detected, but finding them becomes more difficult when foundation walls are hidden from view. To make matters worse, the tubes can be hidden inside foundation wall cracks as small as one-thirty-second of an inch wide. Under the circumstances depicted in figure 2-10, detection would be impossible until evidence appeared in the building itself. By that time, damage would have reached a serious level.

To illustrate the point, let us pursue the problem presented by figure 2-10. When Mr. Termite reaches the top of the foundation wall, he will be in direct contact with a wooden sill plate. If the sill plate is untreated wood, his lunch will start right there. But if the sill plate is treated he may go around it. If he goes to the left, his route to floor framing material will remain undetected under the concrete slab. If he goes to the right, there is a slight detection opportunity as his shelter tube crosses the sill plate. Once the termite enters floor framing material his feeding habits will prevent us from detecting him for some time.

Considering the subterranean termite's need

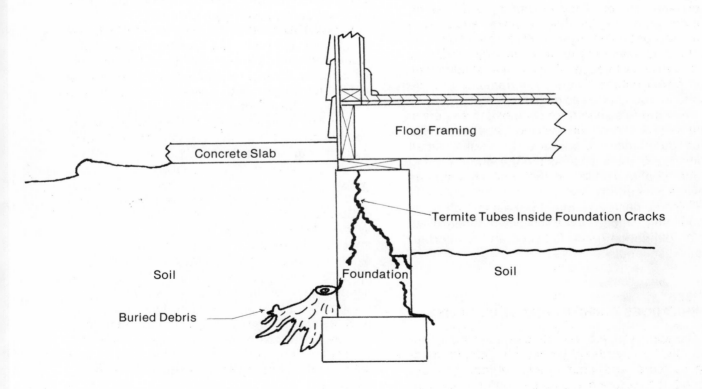

Floor Framing

Concrete Slab

Termite Tubes Inside Foundation Cracks

Soil   Foundation   Soil

Buried Debris

TERMITE INFESTATION THROUGH FOUNDATION CRACKS

FIG 2-10

for soil contact, little need be said about placing wooden structural members directly in the ground. We can also go a long way toward preventing subterranean termite attack if we use house building methods which frustrate shelter tube construction. Such construction methods are addressed in Chapter 4.

Drywood termites build tubes for passage from one piece of wood to another, but these tubes are distinctly different from the subterranean's shelter tubes. While subterranean shelter tubes are frequently long and elaborate, the drywood termite's tubes are more like covered bridges that span short distances. Drywood termite tubes are normally constructed of well-formed fecal pellets glued together.

Dampwood termites do not build shelter tubes at all.

TERMITES EAT CELLULOSE

Termites consume more than just wood, they eat almost anything containing cellulose and gnaw through non-cellulose material in search of food and shelter. They devour piles of paper, cotton, cloth, rug bindings, books, adobe wall material containing straw, dead roots, and building timbers. In searching for food underground, they will even chew through rubber-insulated telephone and power cables. Some subterraneans may be found in wood buried as deep as 20 feet.

The termite's search for cellulose is so persistent that most common caulking materials provide little deterrence to passage. In sealing small cracks and voids against termite entry, roofing grade coal-tar pitch or rubberoid bituminous sealers are quite effective.

To some degree, termites will eat into all types of building lumber. Of the varieties routinely available, foundation grade redwood and juniper are least susceptible to attack.

WHAT DOES TERMITE DAMAGE LOOK LIKE?

The appearance of termite damage varies considerbly. It depends on the termite type, its feeding patterns, and what is left behind. As mentioned, the picture can also be confused by non-related circumstances such as decay and other insect activity.

SUBTERRANEAN TERMITE FEEDING PATTERNS — Once subterranean termites enter structural wood, no sign of infestation will be found on the board's exterior. As a result, the first indication of damage is often a sag or structural failure.

Figure 2-11 depicts what subterranean termite damage looks like when the front face is removed from an infested board. The general feeding pattern is from right to left and parallel with the wood grain. On the right, we see the soft wood between growth rings (spring growth) has been eaten away. The harder summer growth rings remain more intact although they have been worked on too.

Subterraneans inflict more damage than other types because they prefer soft wood and eat more of it. Consequently, they are most damaging to lumber made from second growth trees. (Second growth trees contain more soft wood than old growth. This point is covered in more detail by Chapter 3.)

DAMPWOOD TERMITE FEEDING PATTERNS — Figure 2-12 is an overhead view of dampwood termites working on a plywood floor. Though the wood grain direction is difficult to see because of rot, the feeding trend is again in the soft wood and parallel with the grain.

DRYWOOD TERMITE FEEDING PATTERNS— The attack methods and feeding habits of drywood termites are significantly different from either dampwood or subterraneans. These unusual habits provide us with valuable information in identifying the insect.

Drywood termites prefer feeding on the harder heartwood and summer growth. Their feeding patterns cut across the wood grain rather than moving parallel with it. Additionally, their living and working spaces form pockets in the wood that are connected by a series of passageways.

SUBTERRANEAN TERMITE LEAVINGS — When identifying termite types, some of the most important clues are found in the form of insect excrement and other leavings. Subterraneans retain their leavings inside infested boards and deposit them on the wall and floor areas of all living and working spaces. Their feces consist of undigested soil and cellulose, found in the form of gray and brown specks. The specks are nondescript when compared with the well-formed fecal pellets left by dampwood and drywood termites.

DAMPWOOD TERMITE LEAVINGS — Dampwood termites cover much of their living and working space with well-formed fecal pellets as indicated by figure 2-12.

CLASSIC TERMITE DAMAGE

FIG 2-11

WORKING TERMITES

FIG 2-12

DRYWOOD TERMITE LEAVINGS — Some fecal pellets are retained inside the drywood termite's living and working spaces but most are pushed out through the humidity control holes. Unlike dampwood termite fecal pellets, the drywood pellets have an indented or concave surface and pellet piles are often found outside infested boards. Some pellets may also be found plugging humidity control holes along with the paper-thin secretion which normally seals the holes.

COLONY MOVEMENT

Significant subterranean termite colony movement occurs in northern climates during seasonal temperature changes. Commonly, colonies spend winter months below the frost line unless they have access to buildings with heated basement areas. In the spring, subterraneans move nearer the ground surface. Dampwood and drywood termite colonies tend to remain in infested buildings all year.

SWARMING CAN TAKE PLACE ANYTIME

In completing a phase of the insects' reproductive cycle, many sexually mature termites leave the parent nest each year. This phenomenon is called swarming and involves only new adults with wings. Unlike other colony members, who are blind and avoid light, the new kings and queens can see and are attracted to strong light sources. When the parent nest is located in a building, swarming tends to be toward outside doors and windows. At night, swarming termites are attracted by artificial light.

The insects' wings are used for a one time flight to new nesting areas. Mate-pairing follows the flight, but not until individuals have broken off their wings. Since building exits are the attraction points, discarded wings are often found in piles or concentrated in one area. Note the wings in figures 2-13 and 2-14. In figure 2-13, the exiting adults were attracted by outside light showing through a crack

DISCARDED WINGS

FIG 2-13

DISCARDED TERMITE WINGS

FIG 2-14

beside the floor joists. The night light above the sink attracted the swarming termites in figure 2-14.

Swarming normally takes place during mid to late summer but the eastern subterranean swarms in the spring.

In particularly warm buildings or those with heated basements, swarming can happen even during winter months. When swarming occurs in cold months and the area under the building is unheated, it is a good bet we are dealing with dampwood or drywood termites. If the basement is heated we may have one, or all three types on our hands.

ANTS SWARM TOO

The sexual adults of many ant species also go through a swarming process. Ant and termite swarms are similar in many respects and casual observation of the event can lead to some confusion. But careful examination of the evidence will eliminate doubt over the insect's identity.

If swarming evidence is found soon after the event and located in an otherwise clean area, the story is easy to read, as in figure 2-14. Unfortunately, the problem presented by figure 2-13 is more typical. In that case, swarming evidence was discovered only after ceiling panels were removed during an inspection for carpenter ants.

The story told by figure 2-13 was analyzed as follows:

1. All wings and other leavings were collected, examined under a magnifying glass, and labeled for future reference. Additional evidence was discovered inside, outside, and under the structure.
2. Some wings and other leavings were more deteriorated than others, indicating the area had been in use by both ants and termites for years.
3. Incidental to the discovery presented by figure 2-13, a dampwood colony was located thirty feet from the swarming evidence. The carpenter ant colony was found in floor joists about ten feet away.
4. About half of the wings were termite and the

rest were from ants as determined by wing structure, figure 2-15.

OUTSIDE SWARMS

Swarming evidence outside a building is no reason to panic, but it is wise to find out where the insects came from. We are concerned with the parent nest location because destructive workers range out from there. When swarming termites emerge from the ground it is possible, but by no means certain, that nearby buildings are infested. On the other hand, termites may live in buried wood for years without attacking surrounding houses. If our foundation is well-designed and properly maintained, we may have little need for concern.

However, we should do our best to make certain of two things. First, be sure the critters are not dining on the house already. Secondly, locate all structural conditions which could allow future infestation. Chapters 4, 5 and 6 are designed to help with both determinations.

POWDER POST TERMITE

Before leaving the subject of termites, we should mention one other point of potential con-

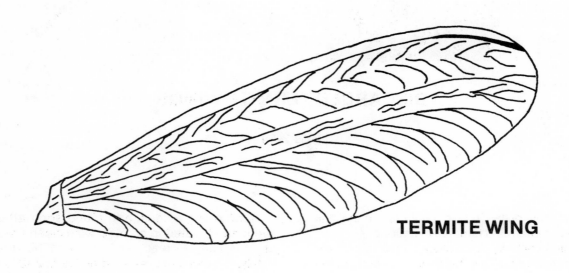

TERMITE WING

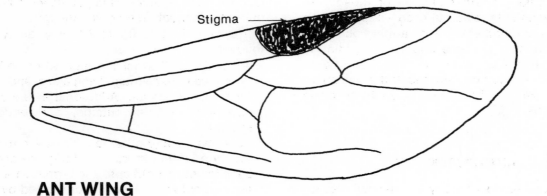

Stigma

ANT WING

FIG 2-15

fusion. Some years ago a drywood termite which primarily attacks hardwoods entered the United States. Dubbed the powder post termite, it commonly infests furniture, books, stationery, dry goods, and occasionally building timbers. Its colonies are relatively small and always found inside buildings. The insect is normally limited to the southeastern part of the country and has many characteristics in common with other drywood termites. The damage inflicted on wood has a different appearance, however. In this case, wood is reduced to a finely packed powder and has an internal appearance much the same as a board under attack by powder post *beetles.* Powder post termites are not to be confused with powder post beetles because they are completely different insects.

We can determine whether we are dealing with powder post termites or powder post beetles by examining the exterior wood surfaces. If the culprit is a powder post beetle, the wood surface will be "shot" with pinhead-size holes as in figure 2-16. If such holes are absent, our invader is most likely the powder post termite.

WHAT TO DO ABOUT TERMITES

By simple mechanical methods, homeowners can frustrate the life cycle needs of most termites.

SUBTERRANEAN — With subterranean termites, the objective is to keep them in the ground and away from our homes. As Chapter 4 points out, some building methods naturally frustrate subterranean termite shelter tube construction. And we can keep the insects out by conscientious maintenance and inspection programs as outlined in Chapters 5 and 6.

Where mechanical means are not completely satisfactory, as in the case of building design deficiencies, Chapter 7 provides guidance on chemical use.

DAMPWOOD — Controlling dampwood termites is not quite so difficult as dealing with the other two types. Dry up all the wood in the house, keep it dry, and dampwood termites will simply die. Drying the wood also includes redesigning areas where wood gains moisture from the soil.

DRYWOOD — First we must prevent drywood termites from entering the house in construction lumber. That is best accomplished through careful examination of the wood prior to use. We should also guard against bringing the insects into our homes through infested firewood or furniture.

For buildings already under attack, the infested wood must be removed or chemically treated.

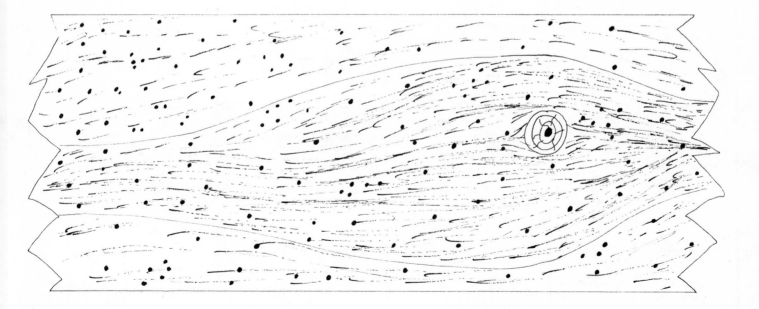

WOOD SHOT WITH POWDER POST BEETLE HOLES

FIG 2-16

SUMMARY OF MAJOR TERMITE INDENTIFICATION POINTS

CHARACTERISTICS	SUBTERRANEAN	DRYWOOD	DAMPWOOD
Builds shelter tubes	Yes	Minor point (see text)	No
Has a worker caste	Yes	No, nymphs do the work	No, nymphs do the work
Color of reproductives	Black, dark gray or yellowish	Light yellow, dark brown or blackish with reddish heads	Dark brown or with large dark reddish brown heads
Soldiers have teeth	No	Yes	No
Workers have secretion pore	Yes	No worker as such	No worker as such
Dark brown spots on nymph's body	No	No	Yes
Water source	Soil	Food and air	Damp wood and sometimes soil
Humidity control holes in infested wood	No	Yes	No
Feeding habits	With the grain consuming primarily soft spring growth and sapwood	Across the grain with passageways between larger feeding pockets, preferring summer growth and heartwood	With the grain consuming primarily soft spring growth and sapwood
Leavings	Gray and brown specks of undigested soil and cellulose, found on the walls and floors of all living spaces	Some well-formed fecal pellets with concave surfaces retained in work and living spaces, most pellets pushed through humidity control holes	Living and working spaces packed with well-formed fecal pellets
Swarming	Summer months, may swarm in winter from warm basements, Eastern Subterraneans swarm in spring	Summer months, may swarm from warm buildings anytime	Summer months, may swarm from warm buildings anytime

POWDER POST BEETLES

(To entomologists, "powder post beetles" are specific species which primarily attack hardwoods. In commonly available literature and Department of Agriculture bulletins, the term refers to all beetles causing structural damage to wood buildings. In this book, the term "powder post beetle" is used in its most general application.)

Beetles constitute a vast world encompassing over a quarter of a million species. Specialists on wood-boring types contend with many variations between thousands of species. Some are short and oval while others are long and slender. Their reproductive and developmental habits differ as much as their appearance. Food choices are even more diversified. Some penetrate only the tree bark while others bore clear through the sapwood and devour heartwood. Some digest wood and others don't. Some survive well in wood with a low moisture content while others prefer damper environments. Some eat only hardwood lumber and others dine exclusively on soft woods. Some bore into almost anything, including lead cable shielding, in search of cellulose material. Entomologists commonly spend a lifetime studying such variables.

As homeowners, we view the beetle world quite differently. We need to know what structural damage they cause and how to deal with them. In examining the beetle's life cycle, we begin to understand why powder post beetles threaten the structural integrity of our homes.

THE BEETLE'S LIFE CYCLE

EGG LAYING — After fertilization, the adult female selects suitable depositories for egg development. Depending on her species, she may place eggs on logs, in excavations into the bark, or even bore deep into the wood itself.

If the female belongs to the Lyctidae group, she inserts a slender egg-laying tube into the cells of hardwoods. The cells of coniferous or softwood trees are not large enough to accommodate her egg-laying tube. When eggs are deposited directly into the wood cells, infestations may go undetected until interior fibers are completely destroyed by beetle larvae.

If beetles bore into a log to deposit eggs, some surface evidence normally remains. Note the powdered wood accumulations on the lower half of the log in figure 2-17. Grubs also cause borings after they have hatched on log surfaces. But the

POWDER POST BEETLE INFESTED LOG

FIG 2-17

point to remember from such evidence is that an attack has begun. In fact, most powder post beetle infestations originate in the forest, long before logs are milled into construction lumber. The powder post beetles, compared with a pin head in figure 2-18, were responsible for the attack shown in figure 2-17.

THE GRUB STAGE — Following a suitable incubation period, eggs hatch into larvae or grubs and the insects do most of their wood-destroying work during this pre-adult stage.

In some species, beetles remain as grubs for only a few weeks. In other cases, one generation of grubs may work on infested wood for as long as 17 years. Grubs remain under the surface and reduce wood fibers to powder as long as environmental conditions allow species survival.

THE ADULT STAGE — Grubs enter a pupa form while developing into adults. Adults then chew to the surface and begin mating activity. The shorter the time spent as grubs, the more frequently adult emergence cycles take place. Surfacing adults present a detection opportunity because fresh evidence appears around the emergence holes.

A tough body armor covers adults including shields over their delicate flight wings. For most beetles, the shields become flight obstructions because they must be held forward and away from the flight wings. In spite of that, some beetles fly for miles in search of food and suitable propagation areas.

When viewed from the top, the heads of some species are almost invisible because of a covering hood. The powder post beetles in figure 2-18 are hooded.

FOOD REQUIREMENTS — The predominant physical characteristic of the grubs and adults is a large and devouring mouth. Their nourishment needs dictate what wood types are susceptible to attack and food location determines what wood parts will be eaten.

Some species do not digest cellulose material; they only tear fibers apart while searching for starch or sugar concentrations. Normally, sapwood is the most susceptible to such feeding activity. Starch and sugar feeding beetles cause the greatest damage because they destroy so

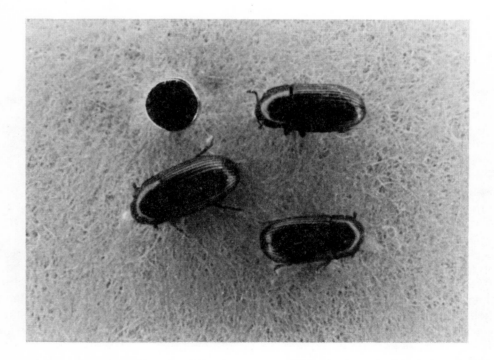

POWDER POST BEETLES

FIG 2-18

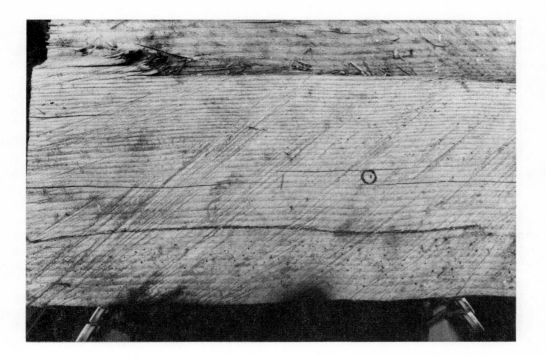

POWDER POST BEETLE INFESTED WOOD

FIG 2-19

much wood in search of digestible food.

The second most damaging species are those which actually digest wood fibers.

Third in the order of damage caused are those that excavate wood only to build homes and grow food like the Ambrosia group. In this case, wood is only damaged by small tunnels which may penetrate through the sapwood and 10 to 12 inches into the heartwood.

Feeding by some species produces finely packed powder. With others, the residue is a bit more coarse and resembles very small shavings. For those beetles which actually digest the wood, small fecal pellets will be found in their leavings. Powder post beetle pellets have a more convex surface when compared with drywood termite leavings which are concave or slightly indented. Like drywood termites, some powder post beetles push their leavings out through holes in the infested wood. But where drywood termites seal the holes after housecleaning, powder post beetles do not.

POWDER POST BEETLE DAMAGE

As indicated, powder post beetle damage depends on species feeding habits and the wood type involved. Figure 2-17 showed us the initial infestation of a fir log. About a year later, the log was halved lengthwise to expose beetle activity inside. Figure 2-19 presents a 36-inch section of the log and gives some appreciation of the damage inflicted.

Generally, powder post beetle borings are oriented perpendicular to the wood grain as in figure 2-19. The circle in the picture is drawn around an adult powder post beetle and the line on the log separates sapwood from heartwood. The sapwood, which is below the line, has been literally peppered with pinhead-size holes. No borings or emergence holes are found in the heartwood, indicating that this particular powder post beetle does not dine on Douglas fir heartwood.

If we milled the log at this point, the infestation would have little impact on the lumber's struc-

POWDER POST BEETLE DAMAGE

FIG 2-20

AMBROSIA BEETLE INFESTATION

FIG 2-21

tural strength. However, if the insect's work continued much longer, such lumber would be of little use except as firewood.

Figure 2-20 shows what happens to lumber after years of powder post beetle activity. Visual inspection gave no indication of the board's interior condition, but light hammer taps along its length produced slightly hollow sounds. One solid blow to the edge exposed the photographed damage.

Powder post beetles attack more than just building structures. I know of one case during the prohibition era where a moonshiner stored whiskey barrels in his basement. Eventually the barrels began to leak because insects were working on the wood. The distiller spent hours whittling miniature plugs to repair damage caused by what he called "Whiskey Drinkin' Bugs." His problem insects were likely beetles of the Ambrosia or Bostrichidae groups, as both are attracted to liquor barrels.

Figure 2-21 presents the classic appearance of Ambrosia Beetle infestation. The flame-shaped stains around excavation holes are brown to bluish in color and are caused by Ambrosia fungus. If the stains are not present, you are dealing with some other beetle family.

PREVENTATIVE MEASURES

Reducing whole logs to rough-cut lumber is an initial step in the milling process. Before uniformly dimensioned boards can be produced, the rough-cut lumber must be dried. In the drying process, we have our first practical opportunity to eliminate powder post beetle infestations.

AIR-DRYING — Proper air-drying methods reduce lumber moisture content below 20 percent. Under normal conditions, the wood in our homes remains below that level and that prevents fungus growth. Without fungus growth, the basic survival needs of wood-boring Ambrosia Beetles are frustrated. But many other species live quite well in dry wood and some thrive in moisture levels as low as 10 percent. So unless we know exactly what bug we are dealing with, air-drying is not a very effective way to combat the problem.

KILN-DRYING — Kiln-drying has many advantages over simple air-drying methods, but the equipment is expensive and must be operated carefully. During the process, all species and developmental stages of powder post beetles are killed by heat. Moisture levels can be reduced below 10 percent as well, but that is seldom done

with construction grade lumber. Though kiln-dried lumber is more costly, it is worth the price in the long run.

PROTECTIVE COATING — Some manufacturers offer lumber which is sealed with a protective coating. The coating retards decay and insect infestation to some degree and is worth the cost if lumber must be left exposed for any significant period.

PRESSURE TREATING — Pressure-treated lumber is highly resistant to insect and decay damage because the cells are impregnated with toxic chemicals and sealers. However, the cost of pressure-treated lumber is roughly twice that of untreated wood and it is normally used only when called for by building codes.

LUMBER INSPECTIONS

Beyond the preventative steps taken by manufacturers, we can circumvent potential problems by inspecting all lumber prior to its use. If the lumber was cut from powder post beetle-infested logs, telltale signs will be evident on the surface as in figure 2-19. We need not be concerned about such damage unless it is extensive or the insects causing it are still active.

One effective inspection method calls for picking apart sample areas of selected boards. Do your digging in areas where insect borings go only part way through the lumber. That gives you the best chance of discovering live adults or grubs. If they are all found dead, fine. If not, you should reject the lumber and address some serious questions to the dealer.

The chances of infestation after construction are greatly reduced by keeping exposed wood surfaces covered with varnish type materials or paint. Such coatings seal crevices where powder post beetles may land and lay eggs.

WHAT TO DO ABOUT POWDER POST BEETLES

Unfortunately, most powder post beetle infestations are discovered after buildings have been in use for some time. And like drywood termites, powder post beetles are difficult to eliminate once they have invaded a structure.

Wood should be replaced if beetles have reduced its structural integrity beyond safe limits. In less severe cases, the insects can be killed through direct chemical application, as outlined in Chapter 7.

CARPENTER ANTS

Brown, black, and red carpenter ants range over most of the United States. They are highly destructive but not nearly so difficult to eliminate as termites and powder post beetles.

CARPENTER ANT LIFE CYCLE — Ant colonies have three distinct castes consisting of males, queens, and female workers which are seldom sexually functional. Males die after mating, leaving the queen and her workers to develop the colony through years of growth.

Ants pass through four developmental stages as illustrated in figure 2-22.

1. Eggs are nearly microscopic in size and take about three weeks to hatch.
2. The larva stage is much prolonged in cold temperatures but only lasts about 20 days during warm months.
3. Young in the pupa stage are commonly mistaken for eggs because they are enclosed in cocoons.
4. After three weeks in the pupa stage, adults emerge to begin their destructive work. Two worker generations are possible each year. Workers range in size from one-quarter to half an inch while winged females are nearly an inch long.

CARPENTER ANT COLONY LIFE — Community life is oriented toward providing the queen and her young with food and shelter. Only mature colonies produce winged adults which commonly swarm in July, figure 2-23. Small colonies contain one queen and very few workers, while larger colonies support many queens and thousands of workers.

   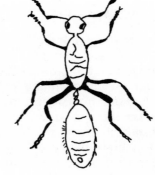

eggs   **larva**   **pupa**   **adult**

ANT DEVELOPMENTAL STAGES

FIG 2-22

CARPENTER ANT DAMAGE — Unlike other wood-boring insects, carpenter ants do *not* eat the wood. They simply hollow it out to provide living space.

Rot caused most of the stump damage seen in figure 2-24, but ant excavations are evident in the sound wood as well. This is also characteristic of the way buildings are attacked.

Usually, carpenter ants attack buildings through damp wood in contact with the soil or wood that is partially decayed. That's because they require some moisture and prefer to work in soft wood. If the colony is allowed to develop unchecked, its activity can spread to dry, sound wood. But the colony will perish if the nesting area becomes too dry.

SEXUAL ADULT CARPENTER ANT

FIG 2-23

CARPENTER ANT DAMAGE

FIG 2-24

Figure 2-25 classically presents the living area of a carpenter ant colony. Excavations are clean, hollow, irregular in shape, and often cut across the wood grain. Where work is in progress, piles of coarse-to-fine cellulose fibers are found both inside and out. Infestations are frequently located in building columns, roofs of open porches, wooden window sills, foundation walls, structural beams, and floor joists.

The barge in figure 2-26 was not filled by carpenter ants but the work appearance is similar. Mounds of wood shavings are often evident under infested floor joists.

CARPENTER ANT FEEDING HABITS — Given the opportunity, carpenter ants will bite any living thing. They will dine on other insects but are particularly fond of fruits, bread, and moist meat. Through observation, we can determine what foods attract specific ant species.

WHAT TO DO ABOUT CARPENTER ANTS

Because carpenter ants require some moisture in the nesting area, they frequently infest buildings that are damp and poorly ventilated underneath. Quite often, we can eliminate carpenter ants by increasing air circulation under the building to dry it out. If you wish to be sporting about the whole thing, you may want to try your hand at "ant trapping".

Ant traps are usually quite simple devices like the one in figure 2-27. In this case, the ants' approach route is over the masking tape which holds the jar and its internal wire loop in place. They fall off the loop and drown while trying to reach the bait, which is usually fruit juice. Such traps are inexpensive and effective if properly baited and maintained.

However, traps probably provide more psychological benefit than actual good toward eliminating ants. Properly designed traps will catch ants all right, but not the right kind. The workers get caught while foraging for food, but it is the queens we are after. Decreasing colony size by capturing workers will help reduce future building damage, but colonies can only be eliminated by killing the queens. More on this point in Chapter 7 (Chemical Control).

CARPENTER ANT HOME

FIG 2-25

CARPENTER ANTS PILE UP SAWDUST TOO

FIG 2-26

ANT TRAP

FIG 2-27

OTHER INSECTS OF COMMON CONCERN

We find many other insects in and around deteriorated wood and accuse them of contributing to the wood's condition. But for the most part, they are simply sharing a common environment with the wood-destroying bugs and cleaning up after them. The most prevalent of these innocent bystanders are silverfish, firebrats, sow bugs, and earwigs.

SILVER FISH AND FIREBRATS

Silverfsh and firebrats are similar in appearance, habitat, and feeding preferences. They are wingless with long threadlike antennae as shown in figure 2-28. Both have posterior appendages sweeping to either side with center tail sections.

These insects range throughout North America and prefer warm, damp places. Firebrats even enjoy the very hot areas around furnaces and heating pipes. Both are quick moving, active at night, and can live for months without food.

Outdoor species are found under rocks, rotten wood, logs, and leaf mold. When disturbed, they dart out and look for another hiding place.

Indoor species cause some concern by feeding on cereals, flour, paper with glue, paste or sizing (such as wallpaper), bookbindings, starch in clothing, and rayon fabrics.

Silverfish are gray and one-third to half an inch in length. Firebrats are the same size but tan and mottled in color.

The good news about these insects is that some species feed on termite eggs and nymphs. However, their natural enemies are ants.

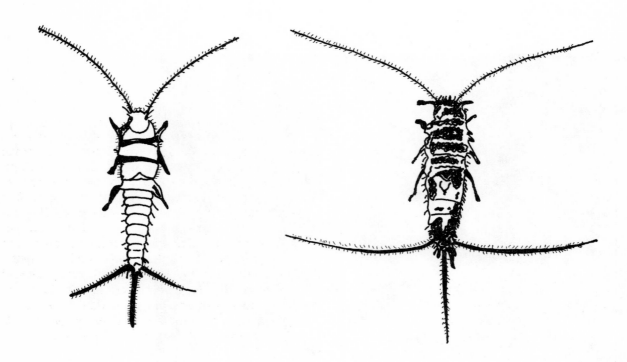

SILVERFISH   **FIREBRAT**

FIG 2-28

SOW BUGS AND PILL BUGS

The names sow bug, pill bug, curl-up bug, roly-poly, and many others are used in reference to these crayfish-related insects. Their bodies are dark gray to brown and oval in shape, figure 2-29. The pill bug rolls into a ball when disturbed but sow bugs do not.

Both insects breathe through gills and prefer damp, protected places. They are scavengers of decaying plant parts and thus associated with rotting wood. They are primarily soil pests and concern homeowners mostly in garden areas and greenhouses. But when we find them around the house, we should look carefully for rotting wood. (Chapter 3 deals at length with wood decay and its associated problems.)

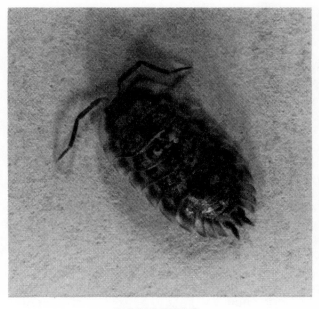

SOW BUG

FIG 2-29

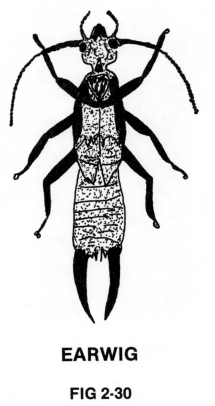

EARWIG

FIG 2-30

EARWIGS

Earwigs do not crawl into the ears of sleeping persons, but that notion is where the name comes from and they do work at night. During daylight hours, they live under rocks, bark and other debris.

These insects are dark reddish brown with a hard shell-like body covering, figure 2-30. Pincers in the posterior area are used for defense, primarily against ants. The carnivorous species also use their pincers to capture and kill other insects.

Some species are destructive to orchards and gardens as they feed on flowers and fruits. In the house, they are generally considered pests, but under certain circumstances they are beneficial. Some of them feed on flies, fleas, and aphids.

SUMMARY

As an assist toward identifying insects before launching into corrective action programs, figures 2-31, 2-32, and 2-33 show the uncluttered leavings of our three primary culprits. A pin head is included in each photograph for size reference.

Figure 2-31 displays leavings taken from a dampwood termite nest. The residue is typically termite in size and shape but not necessarily representative of all speicies. Drywood termites would have produced smaller wood particles. As for the fecal pellets, most would have concave sides if they were from drywood termites. If the leavings were from subterraneans, there would only be nondescript fecal specks present.

The residue in figure 2-32 was taken from the powder post beetle infested beam in figure 2-20. The wood chunks appear to have been shaved off rather than ripped out, and that is characteristic of beetle chewings. If small fecal pellets were present, it would indicate we were dealing with beetles who digest the cellulose. Evidence of fungus would point toward beetles who feed on that. Lacking those other indicators, a starch or sugar feeding species is assumed.

Figure 2-33 is a close-up view of leavings taken from the carpenter ant infested wood in figure 2-25. The wood fibers appear to have been ripped out by a large insect and cast aside. That's exactly what carpenter ants do and that's what happened here. Extensive analysis of carpenter ant leavings and damage is unnecessary. If the nest is still active, we need only watch the area for a short while to identify the working insects.

In the cases presented by figures 2-31, 2-32, and 2-33 much more evidence was available than that shown in the photographs. Had it been necessary, feeding patterns, housecleaning habits, wood type, and moisture conditions could have been used to identify the insects. But naming the bugs we are after is usually quite simple once we have a firm understanding of their life cycles and living habits.

TERMITE LEAVINGS

FIG 2-31

POWDER POST BEETLE LEAVINGS

FIG 2-32

CARPENTER ANT LEAVINGS

FIG 2-33

CHAPTER 3

WOOD DECAY

NEW FROM OLD

FIG 3-1

The decay process is essential to plant life cycles because it provides the required elements for new growth, figure 3-1.

STRUCTURAL DETERIORATION

FIG 3-2

STRUCTURAL PRESERVATION

FIG 3-3

On the other hand, figure 3-2 indicates a considerable decay loss where wooden buildings are concerned. But when decay is understood and we take effective action against it, the useful life of buildings can be extended almost indefinitely.

The Connecticut home of Mr. and Mrs. Jon J. Ekse, shown in figure 3-3, is an object lesson in wood preservation. The house was originally built in 1720 but serves as a showplace of modern living even today. No, it is not a museum and never has been. The house has simply provided shelter for family after family for 264 years. That is not to say preservation has been easy for the present or past owners. It has required long-term commitments and a sound understanding of the wood decay problem.

TREES, BUILDINGS, AND ROT

A tree's ability to withstand forces sets it apart from most other plants. Its strength is brought about by support component organization and the structural nature of its roots, trunk, and branches. Wood fibers are arranged to resist vertical compression yet allow considerable bending without fracture. Fiber arrangement is only a small part of the tree trunk's total resiliency, however. Its real strength lies in the dead but seasoned wood composing the heart area, heartwood.

As shown in Figure 3-4, trees increase in size and strength annually as the cambium layer moves outward and sapwood transforms itself into heartwood. So long as its heartwood remains protected by outer bark, inner bark, cambium, and sapwood, the tree will withstand more and more wind and weight.

A tree's deterioration often begins with sapwood exposure to outside air, which even minor injuries can cause. Potentially fatal damage may be inflicted on branches and roots as well as the trunk area. Because sapwood is soft and damp, it is particularly susceptible to decay fungi and attracts many insects through high starch or

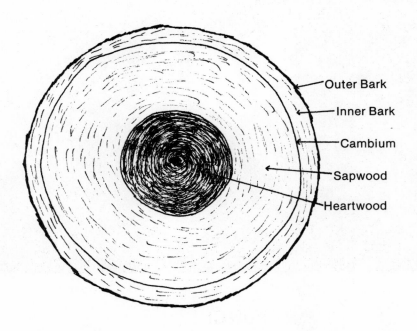

Outer Bark

Inner Bark

Cambium

Sapwood

Heartwood

TREE TRUNK STRUCTURE

FIG 3-4

sugar content. Once sapwood decay begins, progress is fairly rapid as the soft wood fibers are easily broken down.

As decay reaches the heartwood, it is slowed but not stopped; slowed because heartwood is dryer and harder than sapwood. Decay continues however, because a living tree's heartwood still contains enough moisture to support fungus growth. Eventually, decay will weaken heartwood until the trunk succumbs to external force and fails.

Wooden buildings are very similar to trees where decay is concerned. When buildings break down, the same process takes place as found in deteriorating tree trunks. Wood fibers are destroyed through exposure to decay fungi, moisture, and insects; that causes beam and support lumber failure.

DRY WOOD WILL NOT ROT

The decay process requires moisture and the term "dry rot" is a misnomer. Dry wood with rot present is simply that, and no further decay will occur unless moisture is reintroduced. Additionally, wood must contain more than 20 percent moisture to sustain decay fungus growth.

Decay fungi consist of microscopic threads that commonly form tree-like patterns on infested wood, as in figure 3-5. Many fungus types cause wood decay and figure 3-6 illustrates one on which fruiting bodies are clearly visible. In some fungus species, vinelike structures conduct moisture from damp to dry areas and thus expand infected sections significantly. In the rare cases where such fungi attack buildings, the vinelike struc-

FUNGI

FIG 3-5

tures must be eliminated before decay can be arrested. Fortunately, most fungi cannot sustain their own moisture requirements and decay will stop as soon as the wood is dried out.

HEARTWOOD LUMBER IS PREFERRED

As mentioned, heartwood resists decay better than sapwood in any given tree species. In the logging, milling, and lumber marketing processes, wood is often exposed to the elements for months at a time. During those months, ample opportunity exists for serious decay and insect infestation. Even after such exposure, heartwood lumber is generally in better condition than sapwood from the same source. So when we have a choice, we should order heartwood lumber.

BUT GOOD LUMBER IS HARD TO FIND

Along with many other natural resources, the United States has been blessed with an abundance of large trees. From them, we have traditionally produced high quality heartwood lumber for domestic consumption and export.

However, since the end of WWII international markets have placed more and more demands on our forests. Consequently, we are reaching the end of our "old growth" tree inventory and the high proportion of heartwood it contains.

FUNGI

FIG 3-6

Figure 3-7 is a natural comparison of "old growth" and "second growth" trees. The large fir in the center was left standing some 70 years ago when surrounding timber was logged off. This old growth tree stands 230 feet high and 7 feet through on its base. Its age is about 300 years. The surrounding second growth timber averages 100 feet in height and 2-2½ feet on the stump.

Large trees produce a higher percentage of heartwood as indicated by figures 3-8 and 3-9. The sapwood on both logs is defined by the lightly colored sap streaks in the outer growth rings. The log in figure 3-8 measures 49 inches across and contains 61 percent heartwood while the 12-inch log in figure 3-9 is only 25 percent heartwood. Up to 75 percent pure heartwood is commonly milled from large old growth trees but almost all lumber from small trees contains some sapwood.

All of this contributes to the American consumer's difficulty in obtaining high quality construction lumber. The 2x4 being pointed out in figure 3-10 is a case in point.

OLD GROWTH AND SECOND GROWTH TREES

FIG 3-7

OLD GROWTH LOG

FIG3-8

SECOND GROWTH LOG

FIG3-9

SAPWOOD LUMBER

FIG 3-10

WRONG

FIG 3-11

TAKING CARE OF LUMBER

Even high quality lumber faces deterioration through improper storage because decay fungus spores are in the air. It should therefore be assumed that spores are present on all new lumber, ready to become active under suitable moisture conditions.

Figure 3-11 is an example of how *not* to treat lumber. In addition to rain exposure, some wood actually rests on the ground where it will remain perpetually damp.

The lumber stack in figure 3-12 is still not rain protected but the boards are at least separated, allowing drying action through air circulation. The wood is off the ground with ciruclation space under the pile as well. This storage method is also proper for drying "unseasoned" lumber but it should be further protected from rain.

If lumber is dry when received, storage as in figure 3-13 is acceptable as long as it remains off the ground and coverings allow some circulation. To be perfectly safe from decay action, we should store lumber in a dry building.

Wherever possible, construction methods and timing should be oriented toward keeping new lumber dry. When that is impractical, moisture exposure should be minimized and wet wood should be dried before decay can begin.

Decaying wood should be rejected for use in permanent construction, or it should be placed where it will dry out and stay that way.

USE THE GOOD WOOD IN THE RIGHT PLACES

Heartwood from Douglas fir, southern pine, and white oak is classified as "moderately resistant" to rot. Tidewater cypress, most cedar, and redwood heartwood is "highly resistant" to decay and may even be used in contact with the ground

RIGHT

FIG 3-12

KEEPING IT DRY

FIG 3-13

under some circumstances. The highly durable hardwoods such as black walnut, catalpa, Osage-orange, and better varieties of black locust are too hard, expensive, and scarce for general construction use. When heartwood from decay-resistant species cannot be obtained in sufficient quantities for total construction, use what can be found in areas most susceptible to decay. Such areas include sills, porches, lower siding boards, and outside steps. Wherever possible, pressure-treated wood should be used as the best of all choices in areas where moisture naturally collects.

SUMMARY

Unlike the heartwood in living trees, building structural members are almost always exposed to airborne decay fungi and only moisture is required to begin deterioration. The following list of construction and maintenance errors will be specifically covered in later chapters but it is provided here as food for thought.

1. When wood is embedded in soil or masonry near the ground, it is highly susceptible to decay and insect activity. This is especially true in dirt-filled porch areas.
2. Failure to use naturally resistant or pressure-treated wood where moisture cannot be controlled guarantees decay and insect problems.
3. Neglected leaks around bathrooms, laundry rooms, kitchens, and roof areas eventually lead to repair requirements.
4. Insufficient ventilation or soil drainage under wooden buildings causes rot and insect activity.
5. Inadequate eave overhang and faulty rain gutter systems cause decay in the upper walls and soffit areas.
6. Poor carpentry work and inadequate flashing around doors, windows, and roof edges create moisture traps and decay.
7. Inadequate attic ventilation and improperly used vapor barriers cause moisture condensation that leads to wood decay.
8. Leaving grade stakes and other wood under a house and outside the foundation invites both decay and insect infestation.

CHAPTER 4

BUILDING PRACTICES

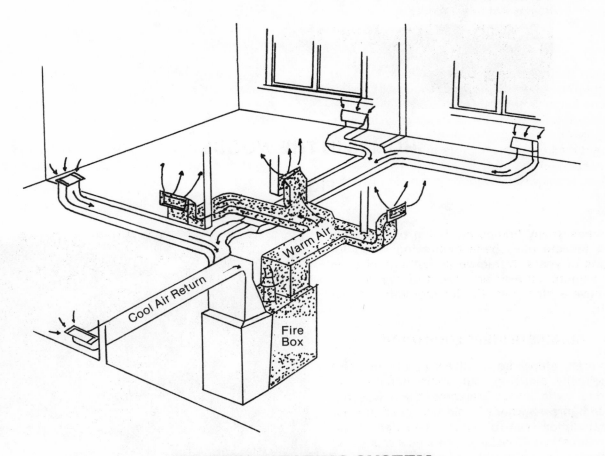

CENTRAL HEATING SYSTEM

FIG 4-1

During the past 50 years, we have made real progress in preventing building deterioration. New building codes, construction practices, and materials have aided us in frustrating insect attacks and preventing decay. On the other hand, demands for increased comfort and rising construction costs have given us some new problems to wrestle with.

Strange as it may seem, central heating plants often add to our insect infestation concerns. That is because basement-located heating units warm the ground under houses and cause insect propagation even during cold months. It is better to place heaters within the living space rather than below as depicted by figure 4-1.

Because we like to live in wooded and subur-

HOMES IN THE WOODS

FIG 4-2

ban areas, many homes are being built exactly where insects have been destroying wood for millions of years. Attractive as settings like the one in figure 4-2 are, we should recognize that they have a high potential for promoting insect activity.

CONCRETE STEPS LOOK GOOD

Concrete steps are relatively permanent and aesthetically pleasing, but some construction methods invite insect problems. Such was the case in figure 4-3 where fill dirt was piled against the foundation wall to withing 4 inches of the door's threshold. Considerable material was saved by simply capping the fill dirt with the top step, rather than filling the entire void with concrete. But the problem created by placing dirt too close to the wooden sill plates and door threshold eventually led to rot and an expensive repair job.

Figure 4-4 presents an alternative method of outside stair construction that eliminates some of the problems outlined above. No matter what methods are used, the following guidelines should be considered.

1. Use treated wood in close proximity to the ground.
2. Construct steps and landings so they drain naturally.

CONCRETE STEPS

FIG 4-3

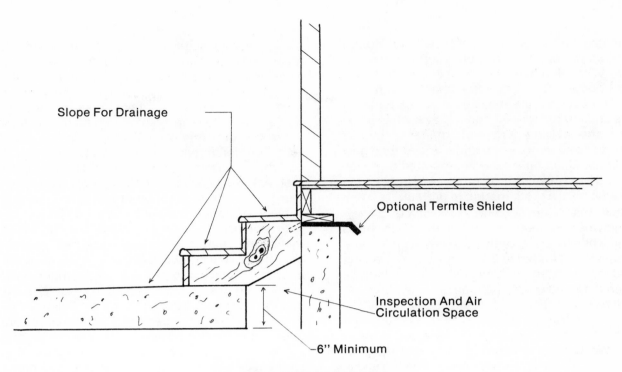

Slope For Drainage

Optional Termite Shield

Inspection And Air Circulation Space

6" Minimum

OUTSIDE STEPS

FIG 4-4

3. Leave enough open space to facilitate inspections.
4. Keep the wood off the ground by at least 6 inches.
5. Don't pack fill dirt under stairs or against foundation walls.

We should not launch into expensive structural modification programs just because potential insect infestation or decay situations are present. But where minor modifications can be made to facilitate inspection routines, they should be accomplished. It is also wise to make more frequent inspections of potentially troublesome areas.

CLEAN UP THE CONSTRUCTION AREA

As in figure 4-5, leaving scrap wood in the building area is an easily overlooked error that is very difficult to correct later. We will belabor this point a bit because the reasons behind it apply to many other errors that lead to insect and decay complications.

Most contractors must propose low bids in order to obtain contracts in the first place. They must estimate labor and material costs very closely and provide only a minimum profit for themselves. Once contracts are awarded, original

CONSTRUCTION TRASH

FIG 4-5

estimates may come into conflict with previously unknown factors that drive up labor and material costs. When that happens, most contractors tend to cut corners to retain a reasonable profit margin. One cost cutting measure involves burial of roots and stumps rather than removal while excavating and leveling construction sites. It is less costly to cover scrap wood under and around new buildings. When houses are contracted by developers, the problem is potentially worse because they also have a profit margin to protect.

How many times have you heard a new homeowner complain about all the trash wood found while trying to cultivate a new lawn. If there is scrap wood buried in the lawn area, you can bet wood debris was also mixed with the backfill material around the foundation (at a depth where it will be very difficult to extract).

Such cost saving practices offer exactly what the subterranean termite is looking for: a bit of cellulose in the ground on which to feed and start a new colony. As the colony grows, more cellulose is required and a new building makes an excellent lunch if worker termites can reach it.

In most communities, there are too few building inspectors to constantly cover all jobs. Besides, if a contractor is going to cut a few corners you can bet he will do it in a way that won't be noticed by the owner or the inspector.

All of this does not mean that contractors and developers are bad fellows. They are in business to put bread on the table and take a vacation once in awhile. Where costs can be cut in order to increase profits, there is a tendency to do so, and the person looking for a quality job should be aware of that. Before hiring a contractor or buying from a developer, you should get to know his reputation by talking to those who are presently living in his product. Real estate agents are also a good source of information in determining the quality of the product produced by a particular contractor or developer.

CONCRETE SLAB FLOORS ARE ECONOMICAL

For reasons of economy and construction ease, concrete slab floors have been popular during the past four decades, but they also cause homeowners numerous problems. With this construction method, wood is often embedded in concrete or placed too close to the soil as shown in figure 4-6. Cracks and structural separations also act as virtual highways for infestation by termites and other insects from underground.

Vapor barrier maintenance becomes impossible after concrete slabs are poured. The intent of these heavy plastic, or rolled roofing, barriers is to prevent ground moisture evaporation into the building and eliminate condensation on wooden floors and support members. Plastic sheeting barriers are often ruptured during the heavy labor required in concrete work. Through such ruptures, vapor barrier integrity is lost and damp spots commonly develop through the concrete. Fewer problems are encountered with barriers made from heavy rolled roofing material because it is less subject to damage during the concrete pour.

Proper construction practices call for 8-inch minimum clearance between finished outside soil grade and a point even with the top of the interior concrete slab. Six inches minimum clearance is required between finished outside grade and the bottom of exterior siding, as indicated by figure 4-7. Recommended outside clearances are intended both to facilitate inspection for termite tunnels and frustrate tunnel construction. The clearances also allow separation between damp earth and wood to reduce the chances of rot. For those reasons, the greater the separation between earth and wood the better. All of this assumes that the foundation will remain dry most of the time. If it does not, for some reason such as a leaky faucet, the conditions again become right for wood decay and insect infestation. To reduce the recommended clearance for any reason is to invite trouble.

However, such trouble often comes about quite naturally unless slab-on-the-ground structures are place on top of natural rises. To illustrate the point, let's examine the problem presented by placing slab construction on a perfectly level lot, as in figure 4-7.

Topsoil must be removed from the building site in order to place the slab on undisturbed ground. If we assume 6 inches of gravel fill and a 4-inch concrete slab, the top of the slab will rest 10 inches above outside grade before the top soil is replaced. That means only 2 inches of topsoil may be replaced in order to accommodate flower beds or lawn against the outside foundation. That also precludes any additional topsoil depth to provide surface drainage away from the foundation. The clearance between soil and wood decreases as the homeowner improves drainage and landscaping over the years. This problem can be overcome through construction techniques beyond the scope of this writing, but those techniques add cost to the original construction and tend to be omitted.

Additionally, concrete slab construction

SLAB FLOOR PROBLEMS

FIG 4-6

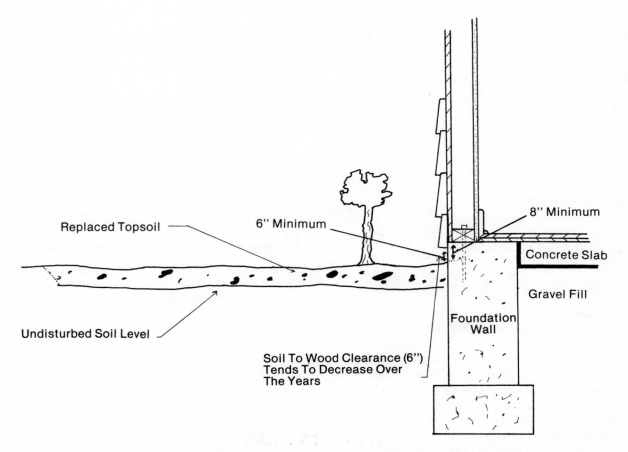

Replaced Topsoil

6" Minimum

8" Minimum

Concrete Slab

Gravel Fill

Foundation Wall

Undisturbed Soil Level

Soil To Wood Clearance (6")
Tends To Decrease Over
The Years

TOPSOIL BUILD-UP PROBLEM

FIG 4-7

severely limits our ability to inspect the structure for insect and decay damage. Since we can't get under the building, we can't inspect the lower floor surfaces or lower wall structures without dismantling interior walls and floors. Lower siding must be removed even to inspect exterior walls. (That is normally not the case in houses with crawl spaces under them.) Consequently, in concrete slab buildings, insect infestations and rot conditions are commonly in an advanced stage before discovery.

Generally, the invisibility of insect and decay damage gives owners of this type of construction a false sense of security. Unobserved, insects have access to the wood structure over the slab's edge, through openings around plumbing, through expansion joints, and through cracks. Slab construction is so susceptible to infestation that many publications and text books recommend chemical treatment of the ground under and around it. The U.S. Department of Agriculture also recommends treating the soil before pouring the concrete.

FLOATING SLAB

"Floating concrete slab floors," as in figure 4-8, present us with the most difficult circumstances.

The hot tar seal between foundation walls and the concrete floor is placed there as a termite barrier. The seal's effectiveness depends on many variables including the worker's motivation; it's a time consuming and difficult job. Beyond that, many physical forces work to destroy the seal's effectiveness, not the least of which is uneven settling between foundation walls and the slab. When that happens, a direct path is available for termites and other insects through the broken tar seal and into the wood above. In that case, infestation will not be discovered until evidence is observed elsewhere in the structure. Even if the hot tar seal remains effective, other circumstances can lead to the same infestation results. For instance, cracks commonly develop even in reinforced concrete when it is subjected to unusual stress.

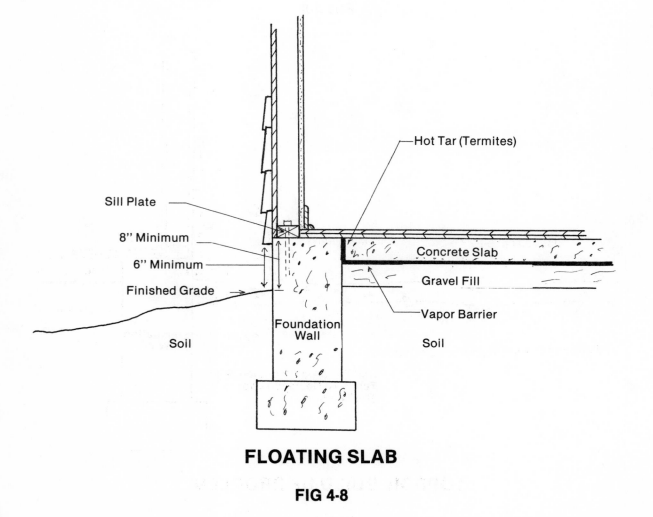

FLOATING SLAB

FIG 4-8

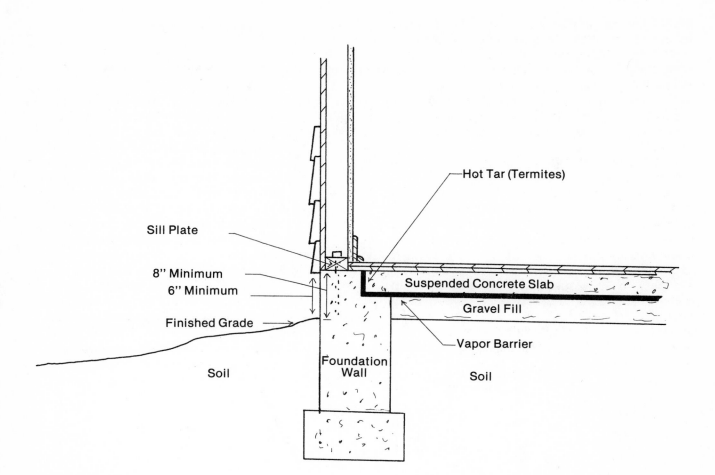

Hot Tar (Termites)

Sill Plate

8" Minimum

6" Minimum

Finished Grade

Soil

Foundation Wall

Suspended Concrete Slab

Gravel Fill

Vapor Barrier

Soil

SUSPENDED SLAB

FIG 4-9

SUSPENDED SLAB

The "suspended concrete slab floor," depicted in figure 4-9, provides a little better protection because the joint design, between foundation walls and the slab, makes separation less likely. However, cracks in the concrete may present the same insect penetration opportunities as found in all slab construction.

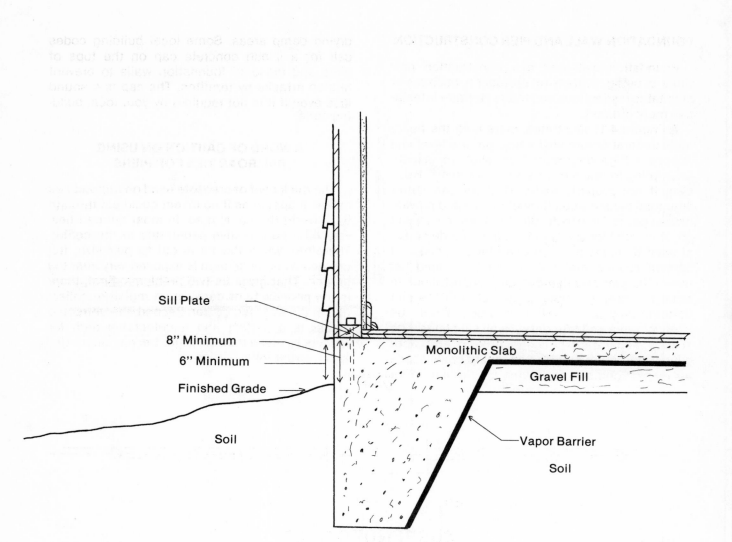

Sill Plate

8" Minimum

6" Minimum

Finished Grade

Soil

Monolithic Slab

Gravel Fill

Vapor Barrier

Soil

MONOLITHIC SLAB

FIG 4-10

MONOLITHIC SLAB

The "monolithic concrete slab floor" is the best of the three basic types. It is formed in one continuous concrete pour, as indicated by figure 4-10, thus eliminating the need for a hot tar seal between foundation walls and the slab. Structurally, the angle formed between the foundation walls and slab is stronger, and less likely to crack, than the joints in "floating" or "suspended" slabs.

FOUNDATION WALL AND PIER CONSTRUCTION

Foundation wall and pier construction provides a better system of protection because it facilitates inspections and makes termite infestation more difficult.

As figure 4-11 illustrates, piers hold the building's understructure well above ground level and impose a high degree of frustration to insects attempting to reach beams and floor joists. However, if not properly installed, piers can suffer structural deterioration through decay and provide hidden paths for insects. Starting from the ground up, concrete blocks should support wooden piers at least 8 inches above ground level. A sheet of asphalt roofing material should be placed between the pier and its concrete support block in order to prevent moisture contact with the pier bottom. Only pressure-treated wood should be used for piers and foundation wall sill plates. The 18-inch separation between ground and floor support structure provides adequate crawl space for inspections and facilitates air circulation for drying damp areas. Some local building codes call for a 4-inch concrete cap on the tops of piers and masonry foundation walls to prevent hidden attacks by termites. The cap is a sound idea even if it is not required by your local building code.

A WORD OF CAUTION ON USING RAILROAD TIES FOR PIERS

The thick coat of creosote used on railroad ties makes it appear as if no insect could eat through it or live in the tie. Not so. In most railroad ties, very little preservative penetrates to the center. Therefore, when the tie is cut to pier size, the untreated center section is exposed very near the ground. That gives us two problems. First, there is the possibility of decay from moisture collection in the exposed center. Second, the untreated center is a perfect and undetectable path for insects to make their way into the pier-supported beam structure.

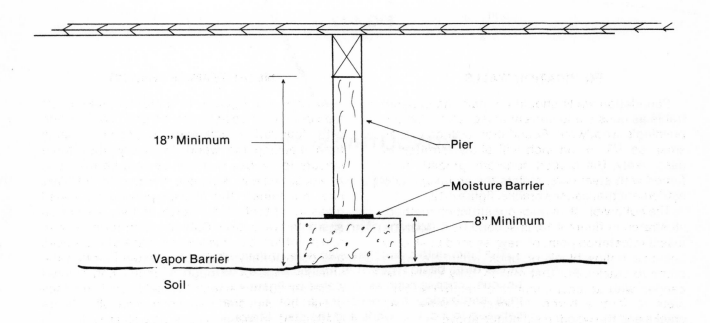

18" Minimum

Pier

Moisture Barrier

8" Minimum

Vapor Barrier

Soil

PIERS

FIG 4-11

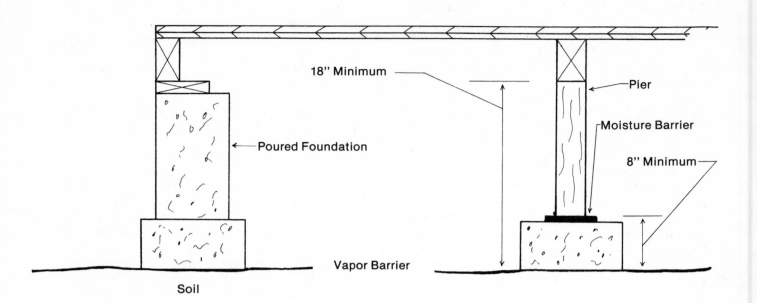

Labels in figure: 18" Minimum · Poured Foundation · Vapor Barrier · Soil · Pier · Moisture Barrier · 8" Minimum

POURED FOUNDATION AND PIER

FIG 4-12

FOUNDATION WALLS

Foundation walls should be made as impenetrable as possible to prevent insect attack on the building's woodwork. Foundation wall cracks as small as 1/32 of an inch will allow termites to pass freely. But poured concrete, properly reinforced with steel bars, resists the shrinkage and settlement that causes cracks, figure 4-12.

The hollow-block or brick construction method, illustrated in figure 4-13, is second best from the insect infestation point of view: second best, only because hollow-block or brick walls are more prone to cracks. For that reason, they should be capped with at least 4 inches of reinforced concrete to form a barrier between potential wall cracks and the wooden sill plates above.

The next best choice is to cap the wall with precast solid concrete blocks and fill all joints with cement, mortar, or poured lean grout. If a cap is not used, the top course of blocks, and all joints, should be completely filled with concrete. If the top blocks are not filled, insects can reach the wood through the blocks' interior sections without being seen.

METAL TERMITE SHIELDS

As shown in figure 4-14, metal termite shields are sometimes used in lieu of, or in conjunction with, foundation wall caps to prevent insects from reaching the wood. In theory, they force insects to expose themselves enroute from soil to wood. Properly designed, constructed, installed, and maintained, the shields provide an added measure of protection. However, they are not an absolute prevention. Subterranean termites can construct tubes on the lower surface of the shield, and occasionally, their tubes extend around the shield's edge or through a poorly constructed metal joint. If metal termite shields are used, they should be inspected frequently. Such shields are often used on masonry piers, as well as walls, and may be fashioned from copper, zinc, or other noncorrosive material.

PROPER TERMITE SHIELD CONSTRUCTION IS DIFFICULT

Properly formed termite shields should extend 2 inches over the tops of piers and an additional

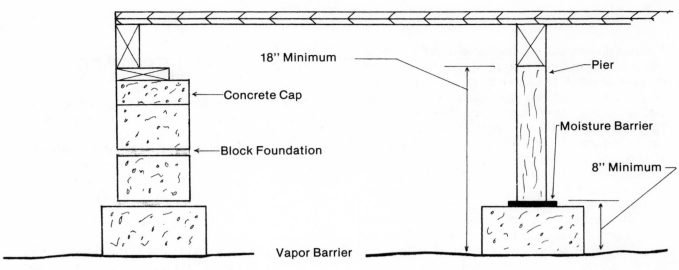

18" Minimum

Concrete Cap

Block Foundation

Pier

Moisture Barrier

8" Minimum

Vapor Barrier

Soil

BLOCK FOUNDATION AND PIER

FIG 4-13

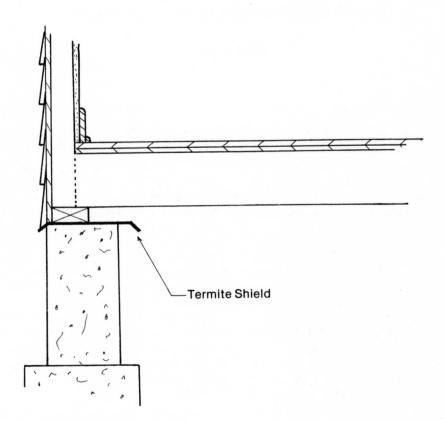

Termite Shield

METAL TERMITE SHIELD

FIG 4-14

2 inches downward at a 45 degree angle. This also holds for the interior exposure of shields that cap foundation walls. The exterior wall extension may be somewhat reduced because inspections for breach of the shield tend to be more frequent. The shield should be formed as a continuous barrier around the entire foundation, regardless of changes in foundation levels. It should be located at least 8 inches above finished surface grade soil on the exterior side of the wall, and not less than 12 inches above ground under the building, 18 inches being recommended. All joints should be double locked, with seams sealed by sweating, spot soldering, or rivets. Anchor bolt holes must be sealed with roofing grade coal-tar pitch or rubberoid bituminous sealers. Common asphalts are not effective.

Given the labor and time required to install a high quality termite shield, it is a relatively expensive process and, more commonly than not, the installation tends to be rushed to the point of inadequacy.

BEAM AND JOIST OPENINGS IN MASONRY WALLS

Where possible, wood should not rest directly on concrete surfaces. As indicated in figure 4-15, heavy roofing material should be placed between the wood member and its supporting masonry wall in order to help eliminate moisture. At least a half inch of air space should be provided on the sides and beam end to allow circulation.

WOODEN POSTS

There are many ways to keep the bottom ends of wooden posts off the ground and separated from direct concrete or soil contact. Figure 4-16 shows a unique innovation while figure 4-17 illustrates a more common solution to the problem. Treated wood should be used for posts; or, at least, the bottom end should be treated. The next best choice is to use wood that is highly resistant to decay.

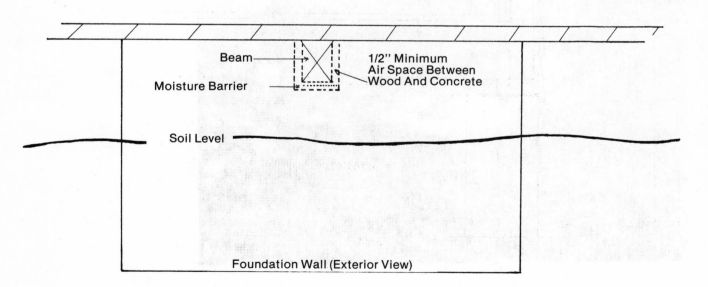

BEAMS IN MASONRY WALLS

FIG 4-15

POST PROTECTION

FIG 4-16

POST PROTECTION

FIG 4-17

USING WOOD IN BASEMENTS

As a general rule, treated wood is recommended for use in basement areas. Wood that rests on concrete floors or against walls should be placed after the concrete is poured. Never extend a wooden member into or through an area in which concrete will later cover the wood. Stair carriages, posts, partitions, heating units, and other load-bearing points should rest on reinforced concrete. Otherwise, the concrete may crack and allow insects and moisture into areas where wood could be damaged. Additionally, concrete footings that extend at least 6 inches above floor level should be used under wood posts, stair carriages, and partitions.

BASEMENT ROOMS

Once basement rooms are finished, future inspections for decay and insect damage become extremely difficult unless the finished product is partially dismantled. One solution to the problem involves setting the wall panels with screws rather than nails so sections can be easily removed and replaced later. The screws can be covered with decorative strips of wood or metal. This method is more time consuming and expensive than conventional carpentry practices but it is cost effective for homeowners who are serious about staying ahead of the wood deterioration problem. The Department of Agriculture also recommends chemically treating the soil under and around basements where finished rooms are located.

WATER PIPES

Water pipes and drains will be considered more in Chapter 5 but several points are worth mentioning here. Cold-water pipes should be isolated from wood as much as possible since condensation drips will keep the wood constantly damp. Pipes should be hung out of the way in crawl spaces, but not placed in direct contact with, or above, wooden members. Condensation problems can be significantly reduced by insulating the cold-water pipes. Electrical conduit and water pipes should be attached to the floor structure rather than being blocked up with material that rests on the ground. Where pipes must be blocked up from below, non-cellulose blocking material should be used. Using wooden blocks invites termites to move upward through the blocks, over the pipes, and into the building.

Where pipes or steel columns pass through concrete slabs or foundation walls, the space around them should be sealed with a dense cement mortar, roofing grade coal-tar pitch, or rubberoid bituminous compounds.

Here again, the Department of Agriculture recommends chemically treating the ground around plumbing that extends from the ground to wood above.

VAPOR BARRIERS

The need for vapor barriers is not limited to "slab-on-the-ground" construction, the requirement extends to all building types. All exposed ground surface beneath the building sould be covered with a layer of heavy rolled roofing material or 6-mil polyethylene.

Figure 4-18 shows the polyethylene application. In this particular case, water up to 4 inches deep has accumulated under the vapor barrier, yet the beams and joists remain dry. A difficult drainage problem exists here and if it were not for an effective ground vapor barrier and adequate ventilation, the wood would be subjected to very high humidity conditions. When wood becomes wet during winter months, it often remains so into spring and summer when temperatures are high enough to support fungus growth. Decay can become evident in less than two years in such situations.

There are several other points to be observed from figure 4-18. The vapor barrier has pulled away from the concrete footing and should be repositioned to cover the entire ground surface. Note also that fill dirt has been piled too high against the footing. At least 6 inches of bare concrete should be exposed where the footing supports the pier. Heavy rolled roofing material has been correctly used to protect the pier bottom where it rests on the concrete footing.

VENTILATION BENEATH BUILDINGS

Proper air circulation under wooden buildings is another important aspect of keeping them dry. Ventilation openings may be placed in foundation walls or cut into outside floor joists. In either case, the openings should be of proper size, and located where they will prevent dead-air pockets from forming. Dead air gives rise to humid conditions. Openings placed within 10 feet of building corners usually give the best cross ventilation circulation. The size and number of openings depends on soil moisture, atmospheric humidity, air movement, location, and local building codes. In general, the total area of ventilation openings

VAPOR BARRIER

FIG 4-18

should equal the total ground area beneath the building, divided by 160. Opening sizes must be adjusted upward to compensate for air flow restrictors such as screens and louvers. Shrubbery should be kept far enough from openings to permit free circulation, and far enough from walls to permit inspection for termite tubes and other signs of invading insects.

FLOOR INSULATION

When floor insulation is installed, the moisture barrier side should be placed next to the sub-floor surface. This presents a problem with rolled fiberglass insulation since fiberglass tends to sag if it becomes damp. The installation technique shown in figure 4-18 illustrates one solution to the problem. No matter what type insulation is used, if it has a moisture barrier, the barrier should be placed against the warm side of the building surface.

A WORD OF CAUTION ON INSULATION AND MOISTURE BARRIERS

Because of hot water use, such as cooking and showers, the humidity level inside homes is nor-mally higher than outside. Moisture naturally escapes through the roof, walls, open doors, and other outlets along with heat. But as homes are sealed more and more against energy loss, high moisture levels are retained inside where water condenses out of the warm air when it contacts cool surfaces. Decay is often a problem where wood surfaces remain wet for long periods, such as around windows in the winter.

Outside walls, ceilings, and the undersides of floors can also collect moisture when insulation material is installed incorrectly. The design intent of moisture barriers on insulating material is to prevent moisture from passing through to the outside. The theory works quite well as long as the moisture barrier is placed against the warm side of walls, ceilings, and floors. But when the barrier is mistakenly placed against the cold side of a building surface, moisture becomes trapped at the point where condensation is most likely to occur, and saturated walls, ceilings, and floors often result. The same situation can develop when two moisture barriers are used; for example, when plastic sheeting is used under siding on the outside of a wall, or inside under Sheetrock along with a moisture barrier on the insulating material.

WOOD ON CONCRETE

FIG 4-19

FLASHING

FIG 4-20

DOOR FRAMES

Door frames and jambs should not extend into, or through, concrete floors. This is particularly true for exposed outside doors. In the case illustrated in figure 4-19, insect infestation is evidenced by residue at the bottom of the inside door casing. The problem here is the placement of untreated wood in direct contact with concrete and very close to the bare ground.

WINDOWS BELOW GRADE

Where wooden frames are located near, or below, outside soil grade, the foundation walls surrounding the wood should be made as impenetrable to insects as possible. No wooden parts should be located within 6 inches of the soil, and the Department of Agriculture recommends chemically treating the soil outside such openings.

FLASHING

Generally speaking, flashing is noncorrosive metal formed to route water away from seams and surfaces where it would tend to accumulate or leak through a protective covering. The chimney flashing depicted in figure 4-20 has been repaired several times over the years, but it still provides an effective seal against rain and protects the wood portion of the roof structure.

The flashing used on the roof in figure 4-21 cannot be seen because it is under the valley that runs diagonally through the picture. Flashing must be used under such areas because the watertight integrity of the roofing material has been broken by the joint between the two roof sections. More and more commonly, however, flashing is being eliminated in roof valleys and other areas where composition shingles can be interwoven as in figure 4-22. The practice is effective but flashing still must be used with rigid shingles because they can't be interwoven.

Flashing should be used to protect window drip caps and wherever horizontal breaks occur in exterior walls, as indicated in figure 4-23.

ROOF SEAMS

FIG 4-21

INTERWOVEN SHINGLES

FIG 4-22

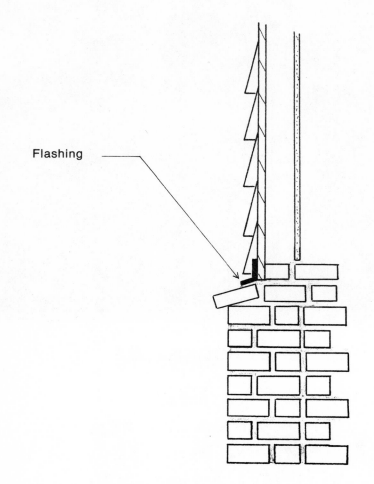

Flashing

WALL FLASHING

FIG 4-23

HEAT AND MOISTURE RISE

When it's cold outside, buildings lose most of their heat through the roof. Warm air not only rises, it holds more moisture in vapor form than cold air does. As warm moist air moves through the ceiling and into the attic area, it can be cooled below what is called the dew point. Condensation then forms on any surface that is colder than the dew point temperature. Tightly sealed roofing covers, such as composition and built-up roofs, tend to hold moisture in the attic area while heat escapes. Without effective attic ventilation systems, dampness subjects the wood to decay.

Engineering adequate attic ventilation systems is complicated by roof design, overall house design, geographical location, and many other factors. The subject is so involved that many carpentry texts devote entire chapters to it.

The roof vent hole pictured in figure 4-24 is presented as an example of an *inadequate* system. In this case, some air circulation occurs at the top of the attic, but dead-air pockets inside the eaves allow significant moisture accumulation.

In theory, roof ventilation systems should work as illustrated in figure 4-25, or as a variation of that system. Air should pass freely through the entire

ROOF VENTS

FIG 4-24

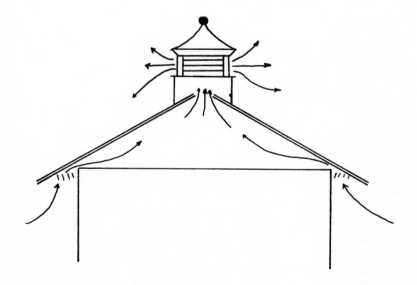

ROOF VENTILATION

FIG 4-25

SOFFIT VENTS

FIG 4-26

attic to remove moisture during the winter months and aid in cooling the structure in the summer.

Soffit vents are an important part of attic ventilation systems. Figure 4-26 shows a common method of satisfying the requirement.

ROOF EAVES ARE MORE THAN A DECORATION

For economic reasons, considering both material and labor costs, many roofs are constructed with too little eave overhang as seen in figure 4-27. While the roof structure may provide the building with a watertight cap, insufficient eave overhang allows rain to saturate the upper ends of outside walls.

Gutters and downspout systems give additional upper wall protection by collecting roof runoff before it can be blown back under the eaves and onto the walls.

If walls are allowed to remain damp, bacteria and fungus will eventually cause decay. The natural consequence of rotten wood is insect infestation, that causes further wall deterioration.

SUMMARY

Under an infinitely long list of variables, building construction is often a compromise. Some compromises seem insignificant while wood is still new, but when decay and insect attacks threaten the building's structural integrity, the compromises become significant. During the building's original contruction, a thorough evaluation of those compromises will prevent costly repairs in the future.

INSUFFICIENT EAVE OVERHANG

FIG 4-27

CHAPTER 5

MAINTENANCE REQUIREMENTS

RECONSTRUCTION REQUIRED

FIG 5-1

New buildings often generate maintenance requirements even before they are finished. Strange as it may seem, significant items are frequently overlooked by, or not included in, the original contracts. For example: we may have to redirect unanticipated water flow away from the house, cold water pipes may not have been properly insulated, or the crawl space under the house may need additional dirt removal. The maintenance list can become quite long under some circumstances.

With older buildings, as in figure 5-1, we face major repair and reconstruction costs due to maintenance neglect or original construction errors. In the words of one experienced repair contractor: "I would be out of work most of the time if homeowners were not so dependably neglectful." That is quite an indictment against us homeowners but it does not imply laziness so much as a lack of understanding. The understanding gap has two primary aspects: first, we may not know what maintenance is required, and second, we may not have an appreciation for the time investment necessary to accomplish good maintenance programs.

A MATTER OF PRIORITIES

Effective maintenance programs demand constant work toward accomplishing realistic goals. For example, we should not put off gutter repair until next year, nor should we allow a leaky pipe to drip past next Saturday. Once we understand how quickly wet wood can deteriorate through decay, and how soon neglected insect infestation can cause structural problems, maintenance priorities normally fall into proper perspective. The pay back on time and money invested comes through prevention of more extensive repair requirements in the future.

SOIL BUILDUP

As illustrated by figure 5-2, serious damage quickly results when soil accumulates against outside walls. The rot shown here is a very common, but preventable, situation. The damage is on the building's uphill side where a natural water flow has packed silt against the foundation. Plant growth has added to the problem by increasing the built-up depth and creating areas of perpetual dampness. Damage in this case has gone far beyond what we see in the photograph. Termites, powder post beetles, and carpenter ants have reduced most of the building's structur-

MAINTENANCE NEGLECT

FIG5-2

INSECT HIGHWAY

FIG 5-3

al and support members to dust. The problem could have been prevented by digging shallow ditches to carry surface water around and away from the building.

Constantly leaking faucets produce damage similar to that shown in figure 5-2. Remember, where wood is concerned, keep it dry!

FOUNDATION CRACKS

Foundation cracks provide hidden highways for invading insects. The crack in figure 5-3 was caused by insufficient foundation wall footing, placement on unstable ground, and a lack of reinforcing rods in the concrete.

In this case, carpenter ant and termite damage was discovered fairly early, but the sill plates and some floor joist ends still had to be replaced. Attacking insects had not yet reached the subflooring or wall studs, but it was necessary to use shims above the sunken foundation wall in order to relevel the floors. Pressure-treated wood was used to replace all infested and decayed material.

The crack was opened wider and filled with mortar to block future use by insects searching for cellulose. Chemicals could have been injected into the soil around and under the foundation as further insurance, but that action was precluded by the close proximity of a well.

In this case, maintenance and restoration requirements were generated almost entirely by poor building practices.

WALL MAINTENANCE

Little comment need be made about ivy and walls after viewing figure 5-4, except to say that even brick walls will eventually deteriorate as a result of ivy growth. Ivy and other climbing plants are also perfect paths and nesting places for insects. Additionally, plants conduct and hold moisture against walls, leading to decay.

SIDING PRESERVATION

Where paint is used to protect siding from moisture, it must be periodically touched up or redone to remain effective. Where metal or composition siding is used, remember it is there to protect the inner wall structure and must be maintained. Corrective action should be taken whenever it becomes evident that siding is no longer serving its intended function.

MAINTENANCE NEGLECT

FIG 5-4

MAINTENANCE NEGLECT

FIG 5-5

UPPER WALLS

In figure 5-5, the upper wall shows signs of saturation from above due to inadequate eave overhang and gutter system deterioration. When the siding was removed to inspect the inner walls, significant wood decay and termite damage was discovered. Structural repairs were costly and could have been prevented through proper construction techniques and maintenance attention.

SOFFITS

Properly vented soffit areas, under overhanging eaves, assist air movement through the attic and keep rafter ends dry. Note the lack of soffit vents and gutter deterioration in figures 5-5 and 5-6. Damage from that condition is evident in figure 5-7, taken after the soffits were removed for rafter end and upper wall inspection.

Even though adequate soffit ventilation was neglected during the building's original construction, vents could have been installed later with little labor effort or added expense.

MAINTENANCE NEGLECT

FIG 5-6

RAFTER END DAMAGE

FIG 5-7

INTERIOR CONSIDERATIONS

Figure 5-8 shows a floor joist destroyed beyond safe structural limits by termites, carpenter ants, and powder post beetles. Although the foundation wall was high enough to frustrate insects from the outside, dirt in the crawl space rested only 6 inches below the sill plates in places. That condition, coupled with perpetually damp walls from gutter disrepair, encouraged insects to infest some sill plates, floor joists, and subflooring material.

BATHROOMS AND KITCHENS

Dampness in bathrooms, kitchens, and laundry areas causes a high percentage of our structural repair requirements. The floor damage shown in figure 5-9 was only a part of the problem, and in this instance, it was literally the tip of the iceberg. Years of floor dampness around the bathtub caused continual saturation of the floor and structural support members. Serious decay resulted, but the real problem was found in dry wood

WATER DAMAGE

FIG 5-9

external to the tub area and bathroom walls. Termite colonies had found enough sustained moisture in the bathroom area to support their needs without depending on ground moisture at all. Needless to say, the required repair was extensive and costly.

Any time the area around water-using fixtures is found to be damp, the problem should be fixed immediately.

CONDENSATION

The problem of condensation drips from cold surfaces such as windows, cold-water pipes, and toilet tanks should be approached from two directions. First, high humidity areas should be vented to outside atmosphere. Second, surfaces on which moisture condenses should be insulated to reduce condensation drips. Where preventative measures are not totally effective, use drip pans or some other means of protecting the wood from moisture.

REPLACEMENT REQUIRED

FIG 5-8

WATER DAMAGE

FIG 5-10

Much of the damage shown in figure 5-10 could have been prevented by a forced air ventilating system in the bathroom. Condensation could have been reduced further by insulating the cold-water inlet pipe and the toilet tank's interior surfaces.

SUMMARY

The maintenance neglect examples cited in this chapter provide samples of the most common problem areas. Every homeowner must deal with a set of specific circumstances that create unique conditions. The challenge is to discover a building's unique problems and deal with them effectively.

We should also mention that home heating costs are increased by using ventilating fans to reduce interior moisture. But when that is weighed against the cost of repairing deteriorated wood, adequate ventilation is probably the least expensive alternative. Effective use of dehumidifying systems may be an eventual answer to the problem, but meanwhile, ventilating fans remain the simplest and most common solution.

CHAPTER 6

INSPECTING FOR INSECT DAMAGE

Armed with information from the foregoing chapters, you are now ready to inspect the house, but you should dress for the occasion first. Your attire should be appropriate for a dirty job and provide comfort while you are in awkward positions.

The following clothing is recommended:
- — Knit Cap
- — Gloves
- — Kneepads
- — Coveralls
- — Boots

A small box of tools will also be helpful:
- — Large Screwdriver or Small Wrecking Bar
- — Small Hammer
- — Good Flashlight
- — Small Glass Jar
- — Note Pad and Pen
- — Small Can of Insecticide (optional)

If you are particularly squeamish about large spiders, as I am, a can of insecticide is comforting to have along when you run into a big fellow and don't want to be distracted with thoughts of him leaping down your neck. However, don't put yourself in a position where you might get sprayed along with the spider. A lung full of insecticide will make you wish you had left him alone.

Two other items are useful from time to time. With a stethoscope, you can hear where carpenter ants are working, and hear the distinct tapping sounds of the western subterranean termite soldier when it is disturbed. A magnifying glass is also handy for examining insect leavings. While examining leavings, take particular care not to disturb the evidence until you fully understand its meaning. Notes should also be taken for future reference before collecting or removing the leavings.

EXTERIOR WALK AROUND

Your exterior inspection should cover the entire house, wall-by-wall, almost board-by-board. Make notes on areas you wish to examine in more detail later, and list all problems that require corrective action. The notes will come in handy during your interior inspection as well.

Start with the foundation and work your way up the walls and over the roof. If your inspection has been thorough, you will be amazed at how many small tasks you have listed for future accomplishment.

UNDER THE BUILDING

If you can get under the house, you have an advantage over those who can't. Go first to those areas that looked suspicious during your outside inspection. Quite often, simple clues on the exterior will lead to conditions underneath that complete the picture. The story may be told by small mounds of sawdust or powdered wood on undisturbed soil. Fecal pellets may also be found with the wood residue. A sagging beam or floor joist may tell the story. Termite tubes on the foundation walls will almost always lead to infested areas. Carefully examine the subfloor and joists under sinks, bathtubs, showers, and washers for signs of decay. Inspect all wood positioned under cold-water pipes or close to the soil. Test the wood's soundness by hammer taps and dig a bit with your screwdriver. Also make note of future projects like cleaning out wood debris, repairing damaged ground vapor barriers, and upgrading pipe insulation.

INSIDE THE HOUSE

Inside the house itself, you should start with those areas noted as suspicious during the exterior and under-floor inspections. Particular attention should be given to the lower walls in infrequently cleaned areas, such as behind heavy furniture and closet corners. Here again, you are looking for evidence, not necessarily for actual damage or for the insects themselves. Lower wall trim may be removed to see what has accumulated in the wall-to-floor-joint. Upper wall damage will probably be more easily viewed from the attic area, so you may save yourself trouble by inspecting the attic before removing trim from the upper walls.

A WORD ON WINDOWS

Decay damage around windows is common, because condensation drips from the glass and keeps the surrounding wood perpetually damp during winter months. Aluminum frames are worse than wood because they remain cold and collect moisture as readily as the window panes.

Storm windows help solve the problem, but only if they are carefully matched to each window. Generally speaking, inside-mounted storm windows are better at preventing internal condensation and that's where most decay problems are found.

WATER USE AREAS

Look carefully at the floor areas around toilets, sinks, showers, and bathtubs, paying particular attention under the toilet tank and waterpipe inlet. It is difficult to determine if toilet, shower, or bathtub drains are leaking without moving the item in question. Before resorting to that step, it is worthwhile to go back under the house and make sure there are no water stains on the bottom side of the subfloor. Don't forget the laundry room or anywhere else where water is used, such as a wet bar.

FLOORS, WALLS, AND CEILINGS

Damp ceilings, floors, or exterior walls may point out where moisture barriers have been improperly installed. Dampness is often a clue to leaking roof material or deteriorated gutter systems as well.

DRYWOOD TERMITES

Don't overlook the possibility of drywood termite infestation, as evidence may be found during both interior and exterior inspections. If heavy wall infestation is suspected, it may be wise to remove internal wall panels for a better look.

BE CAREFUL WHERE YOU STEP

As you move into the attic, be very careful where you step. Walk only on structural members or well-supported boards. You may want to construct a few walkways just to facilitate your inspection. Here again, your inspection should start with areas that looked suspicious from the outside or underneath. Look carefully into eave overhangs, seams where roof sections join, and around vent pipes or chimneys. While you are at it, measure intake and outlet attic vents to make sure their size is adequate. This is also a good time to unblock any vents that may have become clogged.

DON'T DESTROY THE EVIDENCE

Don't be too enthusiastic about tearing into decayed or infested areas. Remember, your first objective is to identify the problem insects. All answers may not be crystal clear at first glance, but frequent referral to Chapter 2 will help. If you are very careful, and fortunate, you may even find samples of your pests. In most cases, however, the insects must be identified by their leavings, and that can become a tedious process. If your own investigation does not produce concrete answers, you may want to call for help at this point.

IT HELPS TO CALL AN EXPERT

If you have access to a County Extension Agent, he is one of the best sources of insect identification information available. He can also call on entomologists through his sponsoring college or university.

Exterminators are very knowledgeable and helpful people. Some carry entomology degrees and are highly qualified at identifying and eliminating wood-destroying insects.

Don't overlook the possibility of gaining expert advice from your local college or university directly. They are frequently staffed with personnel who are highly qualified at insect identification and familiar with effective control measures.

In any case, your questions should be pointed enough to cause your advisor to prove his points, and it never hurts to get a second opinion.

A WORD OF CAUTION

If you happen to run into an unscrupulous "advisor", he may be more interested in gaining access to your bank account than helping you identify and eliminate your wood-destroying pests. The indiscriminate use of wrecking bars and hammers, under the guise of conducting inspections, can quickly result in expensive repair bills. Don't let anyone start tearing the house apart until you are sure it is necessary. Get a second opinion first.

AFTER THE PRELIMINARY INSPECTION

Now that you have a fairly good idea of where problems might lie, your task may be finished until next year's inspection. If you are not quite so fortunate, you may have found areas that require an in-depth look. If you are not comfortable with removing siding or internal surfaces, it may be time to get acquainted with a few local contractors who specialize in repair work. Ask around and locate those with good reputations. When the contractor arrives, let him know exactly how far you expect him to go and what part of the work you are willing to accomplish yourself. If you decide to use a contractor, get several estimates in writing before the work begins. However, don't expect contractors to be able to give you a price on repair until they know the extent of the damage.

SUMMARY

Once you have thoroughly inspected your home, you will find that future inspections are a rather simple task. You will also find a new interest in potential problem areas and will go out of your way to keep an eye on them. The more effort you devote to inspections, the less time and money you will spend on future repairs.

CHAPTER 7

CHEMICAL CONTROL

In previous chapters, we emphasized mechanical means to control wood-destroying insects because most attacks are frustrated when wooden buildings are properly constructed and maintained. However, a limited use of chemicals is sometimes required. For example: once buildings are infested with powder post beetles or drywood termites, it may be impractical to remove all of the affected wood. On the other hand, when chemicals are used, long-term health and environmental hazards are often introduced. That being the case, we should use extreme caution with any chemical that is lethal enough to eliminate wood-destroying insects.

Effective and safe application frequently requires equipment that is not available to most do-it-yourselfers, and for that reason, hiring a professional is recommended. Professional services also provide a valuable knowledge base, guaranteed success, and assumption of responsibility in case of an error.

Some of the agents mentioned below are under very strict control and may be banned altogether in the near future. Others come under limited restrictions from time to time, but are commonly available for use by anyone. Even so, we should be familiar with the chemicals and application techniques before allowing their introduction into our homes.

SUBTERRANEAN TERMITE CONTROL

Considering the basic survival needs of subterranean termites, they are best controlled by interrupting their travel between the ground and our buildings. By injecting the soil with chemicals, we can establish lethal barriers that are very effective.

Although not an exhaustive list by any means, the Department of Agriculture recommends the following chemicals to control subterranean termites: Aldrin*, Dieldrin*, Heptachlor*, and Chlordane*. Under ideal conditions, these chemicals may be effective for 20 years or more. Tests also indicate that these agents move only a few inches laterally and downward through sandy loam soil after two decades of rainfall and weathering. However, there is risk of contaminating water wells if the chemicals are placed in soil containing gravel layers or in soils that crack severely during periods of drought.

Dursban TC is also effective against subterranean termites.

APPLICATION RATES AND METHODS
(Department of Agriculture Recommendations)
NEW CONSTRUCTION

With slab-on-the-ground construction, the chosen chemical should be carefully mixed, in accordance with the manufacturer's instructions, and sprayed shortly before pouring the concrete slab. Apply 4 gallons per 10 linear feet along the sides of foundation walls, along the sides of interior partition walls, and around pipe penetration points. Apply 1 gallon per 10 square feet as an overall treatment under the slab. Use the same treatment under attached slab porches and terraces where soil or unwashed gravel is used as fill. Where washed gravel or other coarse absorbent is used as fill, apply one and one half gallons per 10 square feet. After all grading is finished, dig a 6-8 inch wide trench around the outside of the building. Apply chemicals to the trench at a rate of 4 gallons per 10 linear feet for each foot of depth from finished grade to the footing level. Where footing tops are more than 12 inches below the surface, punch holes about a foot apart and down to the top of the footing. This will provide a

---

* -- Aldrin, Dieldrin, Heptachlor, and Chlordane are presently under manufacturing and distribution restrictions by the federal government. However, they are still available in the form of previously produced supplies and may be used except where prohibited by state or local regulations.

better distribution of the chemical. Such holes should be closer together in hard-packed clay soils. Also mix the chemical with soil as it is being replaced in the trench.

In crawl space and basement houses, the soil should be treated the same as for shallow or deep footings in slab-on-the-ground construction. Apply 4 gallons of chemical per 10 linear feet of trench along the inside foundation walls, along both sides of interior partitions, and around piers and plumbing. *An overall ground application should not be used in crawl-space construction,* except where attached concrete platforms and porches rest on the soil.

Basement floors should be treated the same way as slab-on-the-ground construction.

Where there are voids in masonry foundations, treat them with at least 2 gallons of chemical per 10 linear feet of wall, at or near the footing.

APPLICATION RATES AND METHODS
(Department of Agriculture Recommendations)
OLD CONSTRUCTION

Establishing barriers around old buildings is many times more difficult because some of the building and concrete are in the way. Nonetheless, if we can establish the barriers, the building will soon be free of subterranean termites.

Our most difficult situation is with old slab-on-the-ground construction because the soil we intend to treat is under the slab. One method calls for drilling half inch holes through the concrete slab near where the termites might be entering. To ensure proper soil treatment, the holes should be located about 6 inches from the foundation wall and about a foot apart. Chemicals are then applied through the holes. The average shop drill is not much use in a project like this; better to rent a heavy low speed industrial drill and have a good supply of carbide tip masonry drill bits on hand. (If the concrete contains pipes or electrical conduits, take great care not to drill into them.)

In basement areas where water tends to seep in through joints or cracks, you may want to think twice about drilling holes in the floor, which could worsen the seepage problem.

ALTERNATE METHODS

Another method requires drilling holes through the exterior foundation wall and into the soil just underneath the slab. This method is more difficult since the holes must be drilled at just the right angle and longer bits are required.

With porches, terraces, and entrance platforms, tunnel under the concrete slab, adjacent to the foundation wall, all the way from one side to the other. Then apply control agents to the bottom of the trench or tunnel. Access panels should be placed over the openings to facilitate future inspections and for additional chemical application if necessary.

A more difficult method involves drilling through the interior foundation wall and into the soil beneath the slab. But if you want to keep the problem simple, drill vertical holes through the slab itself and inject the chemicals that way.

For "old construction" crawl space houses, the same methods may be used as listed above for "new construction" of the same type.

Depending on the concrete's condition and the original construction design, old houses with basements can be treated the same way as new buildings.

If subterranean termites are the only problem, and we have taken effective measures to prevent their movement between soil and wood, no further action is necessary. Any subterranean termites remaining in the building will die off in short order.

DAMPWOOD TERMITE CONTROL

Eliminating dampwood termites is simply a matter of drying the wood out and keeping it dry. No chemical use is necessary, because dampwood termites can't live in dry environments.

DRYWOOD TERMITE CONTROL

With drywood termites, all infested wood must be removed or injected with control agents. In simple cases, the infested areas may be treated with a 5 percent solution of pentachlorophenol, which is also a wood preservative.

In more severe situations, the control procedures are much more involved and call for drilling one quarter to half inch holes into the termite galleries at one to two foot intervals. Then a dust gun, fitted with a delivery tube, is used to inject free-flowing dust at the rate of 1 ounce per 15 to 30 holes. The most commonly used dusts are sodium fluosilicate, sodium fluoride, calcium arsenate, and Paris Green. Openings are then sealed with putty or plugs. Pressure injecting a 5 percent oil solution of dieldrin, chlordane, lindane, pentachlorophenol, or ortho-dichlorobenzene also works quite well. Seriously infested buildings may require complete fumigation.

If local conditions dictate, stored lumber may be protected from drywood termites by spraying it with sodium fluosilicate at 1 pound to 10 gallons of water, or fumigating with methyl bromide.

POWDER POST BEETLE CONTROL

Once powder post beetles infest our buildings, they are as difficult to eliminate as drywood termites. With both insects, effective chemical control requires direct kill methods.

For powder post beetle problems, the wood may be fumigated with methyl bromide or sprayed thoroughly with one of the following treatments: 5 percent toxaphene, .5-1.0 percent Dursban, 2 percent chlordane, 0.5 percent lindane in refined kerosene, 5 percent pentachlorophenol in oil, or 2 to 3 percent lime sulfur in water. Oil solutions of lindane are satisfactory for treatment of furniture and hardwood floors as well. Finishing wood with varnish or paint will prevent egg-laying but it will not destroy insects already in the wood.

ANT CONTROL

All ant colonies may be effectively eliminated by killing the queens; after that, the remaining members will perish. Now if we could get workers to carry poisoned food to the queens our problems would soon be solved, and that's what we attempt to do with ant baits. Some are quite effective, but only if the compound has been tailored to the predictable characteristics and habits of a specific ant species. If you intend to eliminate carpenter ants with an ant bait, be sure the bait is designed to combat *that* insect.

The following chemical agents are commonly used to control ants: Baygon, chlordane, diazinon, malathion with Ficam 1 percent dust, pyrethrin, and Dursban. Pyrethrin is used as a one-time-shot against individual ants. Chlordane, diazinon, and malathion are most often used on foundations and the ground to form outside barriers. Baygon is sprayed around windows, doors, patios and anywhere else ants may crawl. Where colonies are living in the wood, it may be necessary to drill into the infested area and inject insecticides directly.

Where possible, all carpenter ant colonies should be eliminated within 100 yards of infested buildings.

ON THE HORIZON

In the area of advanced research, there are several developments that may assist in our battle against termites. One procedure calls for injecting microscopic "nematodes" into the infested wood. The nematodes used are parasites lethal to termites and the kill takes place within days. The process appears to be much safer than using chemicals, and tests conducted thus far have been highly successful.

Another interesting approach to finding live termite infestations is being used by a New York firm. Using sound and smell, a trained dog detects working termites.

INDEX